ACCOMPANYING
GRACIE

ACCOMPANYING
GRACIE

*The Life, Times and Music
of Harry Parr Davies (1914-1955)*

Andrew Everett MA

authorHOUSE®

AuthorHouse™ UK
1663 Liberty Drive
Bloomington, IN 47403 USA
www.authorhouse.co.uk
Phone: 0800.197.4150

Published by AuthorHouse   02/12/2015

ISBN: 978-1-4969-9450-9 (sc)
ISBN: 978-1-4969-9451-6 (e)

TABLE OF CONTENTS

Introduction ix

Acknowledgments xi

Author's Note xiii

Chapter 1   Childhood and Youth (1914-31) 1

Chapter 2   Meeting Gracie (1931-2) 15

Chapter 3   The Song-Maker 25

Chapter 4   Gracie's Films (1932-4) 35

Chapter 5   George Formby and S. Africa (1935-7) 45

Chapter 6   USA Tour (1937) 55

Chapter 7   A Busy 15 Months (1937-1938) 63

Chapter 8   Time for Change (1939-1940) 73

Chapter 9   Canada Tour (1940-1) 83

Chapter 10   'Trooper' Davies (1941- 1942) 87

Chapter 11   New Musicals (1943) 99

Chapter 12   The Later War Years (1944-1946) 111

Chapter 13   Demobilised (1946-9) 125

Chapter 14   More Musicals (1950-51) 131

Chapter 15   Final Years (1951 - 1955) 139

Postscript 149

Appendix 1   Alphabetical List of Compositions 151

Appendix 2   Chronological Lists Of Compositions 159

Appendix 3   The Draft Text of 'The Curfew' 181

Appendix 4   Chronology 217

Appendix 5   Bibliography 227

Index 231

LIST OF ILLUSTRATIONS
– unless stated otherwise photos from Parr-Davies collection

1 - Grandison Street, Briton Ferry (Edward Beckerleg) 1

2 – 2 Arthur Street Neath (Edward Beckerleg) 3

3 – Organ inside Gnoll Road Congregationalist Church (1935 Jubilee Booklet) 4

4 - Harry at 17 years 17

5 - Harry with agent Ben Aza 20

6 - Gracie and Harry in Capri paying cards 39

7 - Harry and Gracie at 'Greentrees' 43

8 - Harry in a cameo role in 'Queen of Hearts' 52

9 - Outside Doctor Naegeli's Klinik in St Moritz 54

10 - Pasadena with Gracie signing autographs 57

11 - Dinner with Charlie Chaplin, Paulette Goddard, Gracie, Monty and Harry 60

12- Harry's Christmas Fun Cheque 64

13 - Gracie and Harry with Mounties in Canada 85

14 - Albert Hall concert programme 90

15- 'Trooper' Harry at piano with Gracie 90

16 - Family Grave (permission of Edward Beckerleg) 147

17 - 'Billie' unveiling plaque in Old Town Hall Neath 2000 147

18 - Plaque in Old Town Hall Neath 2000 150

INTRODUCTION

Harry Parr-Davies was no more than a name to me until I saw the documentary play about Gracie Fields and realised that the songs *Sing as We Go*, *Wish Me Luck As You Wave Me Goodbye*, *Pedro the Fisherman*, and *I Leave My Heart in an English Garden* were all composed by the same man. This set me about discovering more about him. Consulting the internet, I discovered a web-site and even more importantly was given Gabrielle Bell's CD of Harry's music covering the styles and sounds of 30's, 40's and 50's I also gathered as many items of second sheet music and two vocal scores. After compiling a family genealogy I now started to collate my material into biographical form so I could explore the man and his music set against the times he lived in.

I consulted local libraries for Groves and Dictionary of National Biography. Giving ore personal detail were the archives in Neath and West Glamorgan Libraries and I quite quickly came across accounts of the 2005 Exhibition in Neath about Harry, which Edward Beckerleg had mounted with the help of late Bill Hanks. I contacted them both and they were helpful. Edward in particular provided with copies of material on the boards he had provided for the exhibition. Even more importantly, he posted to me CD's of Harry's music covering the styles and sounds of 30's, 40's and 50's.

Law's book on *Her Majesty's Life Guards Band* gave me further information about his time as a trooper as did the band's archivist of *Life Guards Museum* Cumbermere Barracks, Windsor. The census, passenger sailing and newspaper sections of internet genealogical programme *Find My Past* provided me with material not only about Harry, Gracie, but also about the concerts given by the band. Two more resources proved interesting, but less useful. The editions of Gracie's and George Formby's films were interesting in so far as they put their talents on display, despite being often poor in their musical attribution.

Many popularist biographies and autobiographies of George Formby, 'Hutch', the Hulberts and many more that had contact with Harry revealed surprisingly little about him, beyond the detail of a show for which he was providing the music. The 3 biographies of Gracie Fields and her own autobiography were better here because they retail anecdotes of her relationship with him, even if vague about actual dates. Many of the above books contain factual errors concerning incidents, dates, places and people encountered and the reader is rarely given the source of material. Some are mere fabrication against ascertainable facts. This similarly applies to many newspapers cuttings available over the years.

A trawl of local second hand music shops, such internet companies as *Amazon, Abe Books UK* and *The Sheet Music Warehouse,* has resulted in two vocal scores, about 100 items of sheet music and a number of revue programmes. For details of the musicals (9 in all) with which Harry was involved, Ganzl's comprehensive review of British musicals was very useful. Also Harry's contribution to British films (28 in all) reviewed by internet programme from IMDB was invaluable. This has allowed me to compile a list of his compositions, mainly about 230 songs by sorting out what he actually did and did not write for each of 28 film, 9 revues, 9 musicals as well as a few instrumental works and ballet music.

ACKNOWLEDGMENTS

My wife Mary for proof reading

The late Bill Hanks for his information and website

Edward Beckerleg for help with the material from the Davies family archive. He acted previously in the possession of Harry's sister Marjorie ('Billie') David. and now in Neath Library. Toni her granddaughter has given permission to use the archived material for instance photographs, letters and anecdotes; for his encouragement and liberal supply of other information, including recorded music from many sources, featuring Harry's music;

West Glamorgan Archives; particularly Harriet Eaton for the text of *The Curfew* and other staff of Neath Library; Neath Antiquarian Society;

staff of Kensington Library;

the widow of Professor Rex Meadows (and her posting of a CD of her husband, accompanying Gabrielle Bell, in a selection of Harry's music);

Peter Wilson (Classic CD's of Carlisle);

the archivists of Irish Guards and Life Guards;

George R Laws

AUTHOR'S NOTE

There are some practical difficulties in assessing Harry's complete output (mainly c. 220 songs from all sources). While 2 vocal scores of musicals are readily available second hand, the scores of his other 7 musicals were probably not published nor were those of revues. However, publishers did indeed issue some individual songs from musicals films and revues as well as many individual items he composed.

At present second-hand sheet music and scores together with a variety of available recordings are the best sources on which to make a partial judgement of his achievement. Therefore using what I have able to gather from sheet music, songs records and scores, I have made short comments in the text. I have outlined plots of films and musicals he was involved with as well as giving relevant details in the revues. Where possible I have placed the song in context.

Chapter 1

CHILDHOOD AND YOUTH (1914-31)

11 Grandison Street, Briton Ferry

In the already crowded terrace house of 11 Grandison Street, Briton Ferry, a baby was born on 24 February 1914 - Harry Parr Davies. His father, David John Davies (born in March 1880 in Rhydyfelin, Pontypridd) was a shop manager and his mother Rosina Parr (born 1882) was a pupil teacher. David John had come to Briton Ferry and was a lodger with the Parrs.[1] The young Davies family were still living in with Rosina's parents. They had two daughters Glenys Kathleen (born 1908) and Marjorie (nicknamed 'Billie' born 1911). Rosina's parents Henry and Lucy were originally from Devon, coming from Buckland Brewer, a village a few miles inland from Bideford. They had crossed the Bristol Channel to find work in one of the industrial villages dedicated to coal mining and ironworks to the east of Swansea. Henry came in 1850's to work in the coke works as a coker while Lucy was a glover.

The household was musical. Both parents sang; father later became a member and then secretary from 1928 of the Neath Male Harmonic Society, a local male voice choir. Harry (whom the family called *Boy*) had a keen musical ear and so began to pick out tunes on the piano, even when only 3 or 4 years old. The family often sang songs at home.

In August, World War One (WW1) had been declared and sometime early in the war, the five members of the Davies family left the Parr's house in Briton Ferry to move east. Having been refused the army, David John went to Treherbert up valley from Pontypridd to work in the offices in Bute Colliery. Owned by United National Colliery Ltd based in Cardiff, it employed 120 men.[2] There was possibly a rented house with job.

The Rhondda and Swansea Railway had provided a meandering rail line basically carrying coal from the upper Rhondda mines to Swansea Docks It ran from Treherbert (its connection with the Taff Vale Railway was at the side of Bute Colliery) via upper Rhondda to travel down part of the River Neath valley to Swansea Docks. Neath was connected with its mainline. As it also carried passengers, it is possible that the family used the railway to go from Neath to Treherbert.

---

[1]   1901 census

[2]   1923 Colliery Year Book and Coal Trades Directory.

By May 1919, Harry was ready to start school at Tynewydd Primary School, opened in 1863. There as a five-year old, he played the 1918 popular Tin Pan Alley waltz song, *I'm Forever Blowing Bubbles* on the school piano – a presage of the future Harry playing for an audience. Harry kept on with musical activity teaching himself not only to read and write music but compose his own verses with the undoubted encouragement of his parents, sisters and teachers. His sister Billie recalled that he used to rule his music out on sheets of paper and hang them out to dry. In the family home, if they wanted him out of the way, they would give him a half-a crown to 'disappear'.

The family now moved back to the Neath area to a terraced house near the town centre at 2 Arthur Street. Harry attended the Gnoll Primary School, just round the corner from home.

2 Arthur Street, Neath

He was self-confident enough in his compositional skills as a 7 year old to send to the popular Princess Mary, the Princess Royal, a song/cantata of his own devising on the occasion of the marriage to Viscount Lascelles on 28 February 1922. Typical of her, the effort was graciously acknowledged.

In c.1923, he transferred to Neath Intermediate School, where he continued his general education. While there, he decided that music was to be his career. He not only played the piano, and then the violin but precociously realised that he had an ability to write melodies. The result was he composed a number of songs usually to his own lyrics and later pieces for piano, violin and organ.

Gnoll Road Church—Interior.

Organ inside Gnoll Road Congregationalist Church

Harry was taken up by Seymour Perrott, Borough organist, also organist at Gnoll Congregationalist Church. He had been an Associate of the Royal College of Organists (RCOG) from 1910. *He would take up as much work home for his next lesson in a week as would be sufficient to last an ordinary pupil for a month or six weeks.*[3] Perrott lived just further up the

---

[3]   Panegyric by Seymour Perrott quoted in obituary articles in *Western Mail* and *South Wales Evening Post*, 15 October 1955

Gnoll Road near to Arthur Street across from the communal park, the Victoria Gardens.

Harry despite his other studies and activities decided to consolidate his efforts at composition by trying to get his music published. So he wrote to music publishers, such as Lawrence Wright, one of the main publishers of popular music of the time. Wright had himself c.500 songs and was active from 1915 until 1941 (using pseudonyms Horatio Nicholls and less often another Everett Linton (e.g. in 1926 for the song *I Never see Maggie Alone*). In 1927 he published *Shepherd of the Hills, I Hear You Calling*, and *Among My Souvenirs,* which became international standards. Harry had read about him:[4]-

Horatio Nicholls

c/o Lawrence Wright Mus. Pub.

Dear Sir,

Please find enclosed MSS of songs I have written. I am only 14 years of age,[5] and on reading your life story, I decided to write to you. Could you advise me in what way I could make a living for myself at song writing. You will be able to judge by the songs I am sending you whether I shall ever make a 'hit'. I am not very rich, and am at present a pupil at the Neath Intermediate School. What do you advise my next step should be. Would it be possible to gain an interview with You. I know you are the head of the Lawrence Wright Music Publishing Company, could you get them to accept one of my song for publication as it is hard to find publishers. To help me get a start in the musical world, I am so anxious to get on. You were in my position once, help me now please. Could you find a competent lyrist (sic) *and make him to write words of a song, and let me set to music, do give me this chance. Hoping that my songs will meet with your approval,*

---

[4] This letter and all subsequent letters are taken from the original sources, including awkwardness of phrasing deletions, mispellings, etc. in Parr-Davies collection. This applies to the youthful operetta draft in Appendix 3

[5] This maybe a white lie or error; he was only 13 years or maybe less, if still at Intermediate School!

Andrew Everett MA

I remain

yrs sincerely

H. Parr-Davies

P.S/I know that you are a very busy man, but would it be possible in the near future to join an interview.

He in a few years would meet with Horatio Nicholls and work with him on some of his songs. A similar letter was sent to another well-established publisher:-

Francis Day & Hunter

Dear Sir.

Please find enclosed a few M.SS of songs I have written. I am submitting these to you for your perusal with a view to publication.

~~I am only 134 years of age and~~ I was wondering whether you hold any auditions, if so I would be glad if you would allow me to be present at the next one you hold.

~~If you ca~~ If the songs are not up to Publishing standard I would be glad if you would let e know my fault so that I may remedy it.

Could you put me in touch with a competent lyrist, as my greatest difficulty is finding works.

Hoping that my composition will meet with your approval.

I remain

yrs sincerely

H. Parr-Davies

Francis Day and Hunter would also later become a frequent publisher of his songs. Nevertheless, about this he has a foxtrot played at the Empire

Cinema Neath which opened in 1926,[6] no doubt by resident pianist and music teacher, Gladys Williams.

The Curfew[7]

During his time at the *Intermediate School*, the teachers helping him with the language, structure and music of the piece, he wrote a 3-act operetta *the Curfew*. This was based on a romantic poem, much liked by Queen Victoria, written in 1867 by 16 year old poetess, Rosa Hartwick Thorpe called *The Curfew must not ring tonight.* (see appendix III for transcription of the original text). The story is set at the end of the Civil War. Marie Blanche saves Jack Courtnay her lover from wrongful execution as the murderer of a nobleman. She stops the curfew bell ringing, the signal for his execution to take place. The scenario written in an exercise book, elaborated the poem's structure into 3 acts and developed the plot so as to provide dialogue, interspersed with musical numbers for songs, duets and choruses. This is most likely to be an early draft he provided for his teachers. It would be informative if the finished article and its music could be found.

The model used for the work is akin to Walter Scott's more romantic novels to which mild humour and sentiment are added – as seen in operettas, English musicals and opera semi-seria - i.e. after trails - a happy ending. Set during the trial period of King Charles 1, it is a tour-de-force for one so young. It scarcely matters too much that it is set at the wrong time of year, for the trial and execution of Charles 1 took place in January 1649, not at the harvest time the operetta celebrates. Charles 1 is the assassin named), but he could not have done the dirty deed. The motivation behind Gerald de Maur's murder also needs clarifying. There are other historical anomalies in Act III concerning the priests and Oliver Cromwell. It is possible that the final work ironed them out.

---

[6]   Demolished in 2012

[7]   Some newspaper cuttings refer to Harry writing to 2 operettas. In a newspaper interview with Harry, he only mentions *Curfew*. This does not appear to be an extant copy of the musical score, but *I Hate You* is said to be adapted from *Curfew*. If it is typical, the musical quality must have been high.

Its atmosphere is generally convincingly rural. Despite overpunctuation, e.g. a myriad of commas interfere with the enjambement of the verse, some stilted phrasing and repetitive refrains in some songs, the story unfolds clearly and charmingly with place for dances to be featured. The dialogue moves the story on and the characterisation is clear for each of the main protagonists. Alert responses come from the chorus in a Gilbert and Sullivan fashion. The solos are appropriately effective in mood to the situation. Act III after a good start with an *Il trovatore* setting of hero in prison and heroine on stage praying, rather peters out finishing with a series of historical improbabilities and old amorous relationships being revealed. A jolly chorus and a single word 'Finale' hint at general rejoicings for hero and heroine to end the whole work.

As Harry left the Intermediate School in May 1927, the operetta must have been given earlier in late 1926 or around Easter time 1927.

On 24 May 1927, Harry moved to Neath Boys Grammar School (now Dwr-y-Felin Comprehensive School). His parents must have had a reasonable standard of living to be able to afford to send Harry to a grammar school as there would be fees to be paid. Many a youth of 14 years old at that time would be expected to help to bring money unto the household by becoming miners or workers at the steel works. This may partly explain Harry's persistent approaches to music publishers. It was his way of supplementing the family's income. Harry used to go to quiet places during his life to work out his music including the restful Victoria Gardens in Neath.

Meanwhile his musical development continues. He takes part in an Eisteddfod and wins first prize for piano. Harry made so much headway with his music that Perrott made him assistant organist to Gnoll Road church an achievement for a 14 year old. Harry said that organ playing made him think about popular music.[8]

Perrott then arranged for an interview with Mr J Charles Mclean, secretary to the *Welsh National Council of Music*. On looking at what Harry had written, he was sufficiently impressed to arrange an interview with the Council's director Sir Henry Walford Davies.

---

[8]   BBC Radio interview with Harry by Leslie Perowne in 7 February 1940.

Walford Davies a Somerset-born man was an able composer in his own right, chiefly renowned for cello piece *Solemn Melody* and hymn tune to *God be in my head*. He composed much choral chamber and symphonic works, being a supporting part of the 20th century expansion of British music alongside figures like Sir George Dyson. From the beginnings of his Welsh appointment, he worked to promote music throughout Wales, especially with *eisteddfodau*.

Harry had two local concerts in places of worship in different denominations. On Easter Sunday, the first was held for the Rev. Henry Walker's fourth anniversary of coming to the Bethany English Presbyterian Church, Bethania Street Glynneath, up river about 11 miles from Neath. A well attended concert conducted by Mr T J Cole was held there in the evening presided over by the Mayor, Councillor W K Owen. The participating local artistes accompanied by Miss J Walker and Mr M Davies were:-

> *Madame B Clarke – Neath;*
> *Miss May Davies Contralto – Neath;*
> *Mr A E. Stanaway – Skewen (Swansea);*
> *Mr E E Davies – Port Talbot;*
> *Miss Edna M Morgan (elocutionist) – Glynneath*

Harry played a selection of his own compositions.

This second concert was presided over again by the Mayor and is detailed on the programme opposite. It was dedicated entirely to music composed by Harry, (especially a selection of excerpts from *Curfew).* The words of the song were written also mostly by him.

The second concert was held nearer home at the (London Road) English Wesleyan Methodist Church Neath built in 1869 on Thursday the 19 April 1928. The Mayor presided as in the first concert. I was dedicated solely to his compositions. He had written all the music and apart from one song all the lyrics. It was announced as:

A GRAND CONCERT
Will be held in the above Church, of Works
Composed by
HARRY PARR DAVIES,
the Neath Boy Composer
Chair to be taken at 7.30 p.m. by His Worship
the Mayor, Councillor W J Owen JP [9]
ARTISTES
Soprano; Miss Mary Parker
Contralto; Miss May Davies
Tenor; Mr Roy Hocking
Bass; Mr J Gwynne
VIOLINIST; Master Ken Cole
Organist; Mr Phil. David
AND THE COMPOSER
PROGRAMME: 1 SHILLING
Proceeds in aid of the Church Renovation Fund

1.	Overture : -	"The Curfew"	H.P.D
		Harry Parr Davies	
2.	Opening Chorus : -	"The Curfew"	H.P.D
		The Choir	
3.	Solo : -	"Drifting"	H.P.D
		Mr J Gwynne	
4.	Solo : -	"Home"	H.P.D
		(Words by Judge Perry)	
		Miss Mary Parker	
5.	Violin Solo : -	"La Rêve d'Amour"	H.P.D
		Master Ken Cole	
6.	Solo : -	"Tho' skies that were blue"	H.P.D
		Mr Roy Hocking	
7.	Solo : -	"Cottage of Dreams Come True"	H.P.D
		Miss May Davies	
8.	Organ solo : -	"Melodie"	H.P.D
		Mr P David	
9.	Duet : -	"Serenade (The Curfew)"	H.P.D
		Mr J Gwynne and Miss M. Davies	

---

[9]   Mayor for 1927-8 the programme wrongly gives WJ as his initials, William
Kindon were his forenames.

INTERVAL

PART 2

1.	Pianoforte Solo : -	"Legends"	H.P.D
		Harry Parr Davies	
2.	Opening Chorus : -	"Priest's Chorus" (The Curfew)	H.P.D
		The Choir	
3.	Solo : -	"Harbour Lights"	H.P.D
		Mr Roy Hocking	
4.	Violin Solo : -	"Nocturne"	H.P.D
		Master Ken Cole	
5.	Duet : -	"Dearie" (The Curfew)	H.P.D
		Miss Mary Parker and Mr Roy Hocking	
6.	Solo : -	"Wond'ring"	H.P.D
		Mr J Gwynne	
7.	Solo : -	"The Shades of Night" (The Curfew)	H.P.D
		Miss May Davies	
8.	Solo : -	"Love Finds a Way" (The Curfew)	H.P.D
		Miss Mary Parker	
9.	Solo and Chorus : -	"Prayer" (The Curfew)	H.P.D
		Miss Mary Parker and Choir	

DOXOLOGY

Harry attended the Methodist Sunday School at Wesley Church.[10] He even wrote a march for organ *Tesgar* in honour of the Methodist minister's son Tesgar Humphreys. It is a typical marching hymn tune like *Llanfair* or *Cwm Rhondda*. with a distinct bass line.

Walford Davies having heard Harry's music and music-making at school now started pushing Harry towards the Classics and a career as a serious musician. At this time, further musical education relied heavily on the Viennese school of masters - Mozart, Haydn, Beethoven. The expressive features of Italian and French opera while popular and given to many provincial audiences by touring companies like the Carl Rosa were regarded with some disdain by the British musical establishment. Opera was still heavily under the reforming influence of Wagner.

---

[10]   This is the only overtly religious contact that Harry had.

Davies sent Harry a weighty package of what he deemed appropriate music for Harry to examine. He advised him to emulate the style of the 'greats'. Well meaning, Davies promised to review what he produced after such study. He was beginning to groom Harry for Oxford or Cambridge. At first, Harry acquiesced.

Shortly after completing, *The Curfew* Harry was in London escorted by his aunt for an organ exam[11] taken probably on Perrott's advice. (Perrott had after a lapse of 11 years resumed his membership of RCOG and gained his Fellowship in July 1929). While in London, Harry became acquainted with successful national pantomime impresario Julian Wylie. Hearing his music he suggested Harry write a song for a new musical in its pre-production. Harry responded with a song, *Peter the Pup is Twenty-one To-day.* Unfortunately the production never happened.. Harry could well have responded with other songs after all 6 of them were eventually published.

After many more discussions, he eventually came to a conscious decision not to follow this more academic path. This was quite a remarkable and risky thing for a teenager to do, especially in the 1920's and in the provinces. He seemingly knew his strengths and limitations, wanted to continue with lighter more lyrical works. His models at this stage were Eric Coates and Edward German, composers familiar from radio, concert hall and stage. They both provided light music of quality, admired by their contemporaries.

Eric Coates wrote popular marches, orchestral pieces and songs throughout his professional life from 1909 until 1957, including *By a Sleepy Lagoon, the Dam Busters March, Knightsbridge* – all still familiar through use by radio, film and TV as theme tunes. He used orchestral forms as suites (*3 Elizabeths*) or fantasy pieces (*The Three Bears*). His songs are likewise charming miniatures (*Bird songs at Eventide* and *Green Hills of Somerset.* He used clearly outlined melodies in a well-ordered orchestral or pianistic dressing.[12] This is probably his legacy to Harry, who applied the principle to the 200 songs he wrote. Interestingly Coates did not come

---

[11]   BBC Radio interview with Harry interviewed by Leslie Perowne in 1939.

[12]   Self, Geoffrey, 1986, *In Town Tonight,- a centenary study of the life and music of Eric Coates,* Thames Publishing

round to using his melodic gifts for stage works. For this, Harry had Edward German as a model.[13]

Edward German composed a wide range of works, orchestral pieces, songs, choral and chamber works as well as a lot of incidental music for plays and 6 operettas of charm, *Merrie England* and *Tom Jones* and others. He uses broad expansive melodies that are finely and appropriately orchestrated. His vocal music lies well in the voice of the character and style being portrayed.[14] Harry's *Curfew* is certainly in a similar strain to German's operettas wordwise. Later especially in *Dear Miss Phoebe*, the musical model throughout is very reminiscent of German's style.

Becoming better known

Harry's reputation was on the increase. One of his compositions, *Memories* a violin solo, was played by Albert Sandler, the popular light classical violinist and leader of the Park Lane Hotel Orchestra. It was then broadcast, being played by Reginald Foort, the organist of the Regal Cinema, Marble Arch sometime after its opening in November 1928. (Edward O'Henry organist at the London's Tussaud Cinema also played Harry's music). Another of Harry's songs, *Underneath the Moon in Old Shanghai*, a title reminiscent of Horatio Nicholl's 1925 song *Shanghai,* was sung by local comedian Seymour Collins and had been published.

Harry wrote to one publisher seeking royalties, which were not very forth coming:-

---

13 *The New Groves Dictionary of Music and Musicians,* 2001, 2nd Edition, Oxford University Press – Eric Coates and Edward German

14 Self, Geoffrey, 1986, *In Town Tonight,- a centenary study of the life and music of Eric Coates,* Thames Publishing

Andrew Everett MA

Empire Music Publishers

319 Oxford St.

London W. C. 2

Dear Sirs/

Re "Underneath the Moon in Old Shanghai"

I believe there are some royalties due to me on account of the publication by you of the above song. They are due(as you state in your memorandum of agreement) on midsummer and Xmas. I should be obliged if you would let me know whether there are royalties due to me at all? If so I would be glad if you would forward them immediately.

yrs sincerely

H. Parr-Davies

His single-mindedness was remarkable for his age. He achieved performance of his music, its publication throughout his childhood and youth, coupled with musical activity in Neath, not ceasing in his efforts to promote his own music, his career and finances. It was a sound preparation for the future. He was learning how to organise and work at his future career as composer and pianist. All he needed was a catalyst. He had prepared the ground.

CHAPTER 2

MEETING GRACIE (1931-2)

Harry following on from his earlier forays into the entertainment world decided to try and meet with the increasingly well known and popular Gracie Fields. She preferred the spontaneity of live audiences, having built up her reputation by hard work touring the country as a comedienne/singer and then starring in revues organised by her theatrical agent, her husband Archie Pitts, from whom she was estranged domestically.

Sally in Our Alley

The British film industry was just moving out of the earlier 'silent' era. So the time was ripe for to start a film career. Her first film was with the Associated Talking Pictures (ATP) in a part documentary drama - part musical comedy film set in World War One, *Sally in Our Alley*. Directed by the experienced Maurice Elvey, Basil Dean was its producer with the veteran conductor- composer-arranger Ernest Irving responsible for the music. The film allowed Gracie to import into the film the song, which became her signature tune *Sally*. Archie Pitt with his music hall and stage experience wrote some of the scenes.

Released on 17 July 1931, it was very successful nationally. Indeed Harry is likely to have seen it when it was at the Empire Cinema, Neath during 1931. The world behind making films - all became part of Harry's world up to World War Two (WW2) and beyond.

Walk This Way

After the success of *Sally*, Archie Pitt continued to build up Gracie's career by showcasing her talents in a revue called *Walk This Way*. This had the usual preview tour, starting on 27 July at the Opera House, Blackpool. It then moved on to Palace Theatre, Manchester; by 21 September was at Theatre Royal, Nottingham, 12 October at Grand Theatre Leeds and 30 November at Southsea. It finally opened in London on 17 December at the Winter Gardens Theatre,[15] Drury Lane in 17 December, closing after a total of 149 performances on 23 March 1932.

Revues

Originally revues in Britain were developed by the French actor impresario André Charlot. He put over 30 from 1917 to 1935 His great rival was Charles B Cochrane with 150 popular stage productions, including revues. Between them they gave a wide variety of actors, singers, comedians, variety acts and playwrights their opportunities.

Revues themselves were in some ways an up-market cross between contrasting musical hall acts and some of the more loosely structured musical comedies and operettas. Usually in two acts, each act featuring an average of 6 or 7 individual items. Often in the form of sketches, each act had a rousing finale to bring down the curtain. The material would be built around a company of popular performers, whether comedians, singers, dancers, acrobats. The sketches themselves could be sentimental, satirical, gymnastic, whimsical, musical or a mixture of them all and often included a ballet sequence. Sometime the entire score would be provided by a specific composer, but more often, it was done by a number of composers each writing items appropriate to the sketches etc. The whole of the resulting music was usually assembled and arranged by a musical director, who conducted the resident orchestras as well.

---

[15]　Now called the New Theatre

Walk This Way was typical. Built around Gracie as singer, comedienne and character actor (e.g. as a Pearly Queen), it included Irene Pitts, Gracie's step-daughter and Gracie in the characteristic *The Doll and The Golliwog*. Gracie's brother Tommy provided the comedy and singing (he had a pleasant evenly toned baritone voice) and another comic character actor washer brother-in-law Douglas (Dougie) Wakefield. Added to this were different music hall friends and colleagues. Many of these appeared again in her 1930's films. This was in fact the last review in which Gracie was featured. Henceforth, concert and films were her choice of performing venue.

YOUNG NEATH COMPOSER.
Henry Parr-Davies, the 17-years-old Neath boy, who has composed songs which Miss Gracie Fields is to sing in a new revue.

Meeting Gracie

In 1931, Harry was on his Christmas holidays from school. *I was smitten with the idea that I had written just the song for Gracie Fields.... I raised the wind (from his sisters?) to buy a half-day ticket to London.* He told his parents about what he wanted to do. He would be able to get a direct train to Paddington, joining the train from Swansea. He made his way to Theatreland. Wylie for whom he had written a song earlier was sufficiently impressed to have a word with Gracie. So it is likely Harry was half expected. by her.[16] He recounted it five years later with typical Welsh exuberance:-

Probably a school boy was a new phenomenon in the experience of the hardboiled guardian of the stage door, but he had pity on my youth and shyness.

'What do you want?' he demanded.

'I've written a song that I want to play to Miss Fields'. That speech was meant to be my passport to the great actress and since I had anticipated no opposition, I had prepare no argument to follow it.

The stage-door keeper was not at that disadvantage. He had polished his technique of resistance in the hard school of experience. I am prepared to swear that he swelled to twice his size, making the door literally impassable.

I might write and ask for an appointment with her manager. Or I might send the song by post. Or possibly he might relieve me of it himself and let his wastepaper basket save Miss Fields and her manager a lot of bother. Or I might take myself off to the devil. There were plenty of alternative to my seeing Miss Fields

---

16   There is a plethora of accounts available for this key encounter in both their lives. Many have different details and internal contradictions. The basis for the author's account from the Parr-Davies Collection is an undated (c. 1937) unsourced newspaper interview entitled *I "Gatecrashed" Miss Fields* given by Harry. Much has the ring of authenticity. He gives his age at this interview as a year too young and so it doesn't fit the school record from Dwr-y-felin School. Other interviews given by Harry both written and spoken can differ from this rather fuller account but are often just summaries of the meeting and its effects.

Gracie was in her dressing room. *Our debate had achieved a 'fortissimo' when the unmistakable voice of Miss Fields came down the passage soaring over our row.*

"What's going on down there?" she asked.

"Another of these song writers. A kid this time", he answered, bit I will swear that his form here began to shrink for I could see past him into the passage.

"A kid? Let's see what he's got" Came the command.

It was victory after all, for my enemy became the conductor to the rooms of the great Gracie Fields..... I was shown in.... by the grace of one chance in a million there was a piano in it...... a piano is never part of a dressing room furniture. This was the stage piano, shoved into this room out of the way, because there was no room for it on stage.[17]

A 'long, lanky lad of seventeen, looking half-scared' edged his way into her dressing-room.[18]

"What have you got there, Lad?"

"A song I think you will like." I answered. "It is called "I Hate You"". *Suddenly the title seemed to me undiplomatic, but Miss Fields burst out laughing, opened the piano and invited me to sit down.*

I spread out my song and began to play.

"You're a grand player, lad, but what about the words? Go on, sing up!"

Now I cannot sing and at sixteen my voice was a wretched croak. I did my miserable best.

---

[17] *I "Gatecrashed" Gracie Fields.-* unsourced and undated newspaper interview with Harry, c1937 after tours of South Africa and USA, in the Parr-Davies Collection.

[18] Fields, Gracie, 1960, *Sing as We Go, The Autobiography of Gracie Fields,* Frederick Mulle, p.106

"Not much of a singer, are you, lad?" observed my heroine but I thought she was taken with tune, and she herself began to sing the words, singing them with interest too.

"I like this", she said, "and I shall use it my next film." She kept her promise.

She sent me along to see her manager, Bert Aza.

Having heard him play she arranged to engage him at once, as her accompanist. He returned home, *I was afraid to go to sleep that night lest I wake up and find it was a dream. It was not until a formal contract came along that my parents could believe that I had fallen in with a group of London leg-pullers.*[19]

He came back with his parents' consent to London to sign the contract drawn up by Bert Aza.

Harry with agent Bert Aza

---

[19]   *I "Gatecrashed" Gracie Fields*

This was for his compositions. He had an enjoyable fortnight[20] with Gracie and her husband Archie.

Despite Gracie's keenness to have *I Hate You* introduced as a number into *Walk This Way*, it didn't happen. Harry commented *I should have had to conduct the Winter Garden Orchestra for some time on that particular scene.* It was nevertheless put in her next film He was asked to do a new ballad for *Walk This Way*. *They were very eager to keep me in London, but I was intent upon sitting for my matriculation at the County school in July.*[21] It would seem that he still had some lingering idea of going to University, seeing his composing as a lucrative sideline.

In practice, he did not go to either Oxford or Cambridge University.. *One night, as Harry stood in the wings with me before I went on I said "That piano looks proper lonely out there harry, why don't you go and sit at it?" He had never been on a stage before and was terrified. But I got him at the piano that night*[22] [23] He was offered a summer vocation trial period as Gracie's her accompanist. He took it and the result was he spent most of the next decade playing the piano for her stage act, accompanying her performances all over the world. Getting such a job was for a 17-year old at that time an opportunity not to be missed in a period of high unemployment.

Oddly, Grace did not do any more revues after this one, being on the brink of a film career. She continued her preference for live appearances at concert venues as before up and down the land, but now with Harry as her accompanist and composer

His skill as accompanist

She came to find that he was exceptional. She had an infuriating habit of suddenly changing key in the middle of a number plus her mischievous

---

[20]   This would tally with absences he had from school.

[21]   Undated (c. February/ March) 1932 interview in *South Wales Daily Post*

[22]   Fields, Gracie, 1960, *Sing as We Go, The Autobiography of Gracie Fields,* Frederick Mulle, p.107

[23]   Not professionally, but he had more experience in performing than Gracie realised! He was obviously more nervous by being put in the spotlight.

aims to raise a laugh by trying put him off. He never once failed her. Her comment to the audience was typical. *This is the little lad that mucks around on the piano.*[24] He learnt to play her repertoire of an estimated 150 songs of many different types from memory. He preferred not to sight-read music as he was short-sighted.[25] During a number, Harry was fully up to what she was doing. A sign or repartee would provide him with a clue for change. His prodigious memory added to an enviable ability to transpose rapidly helped him cope with any expressive or comedic halts, witty wisecracks (and subsequent audience laughter) which Gracie felt inclined to make.

His therefore was a unique supporting talent to say the least! Furthermore, he was able to help her become subtler musically, putting it in his own whimsical way. *You're nervous, Gracie, you're singing too loud. Your mother may like it, I don't!*[26] Thus Harry became invaluable to her. He penned for her solo songs for her concerts in addition to those he had written from her films.

Harry's ability as a pianist is heard in recordings e.g. in a selection from *This Week of Grace* there is revealed a firm but light and agile touch. He uses his melodies as a basis for jazz-style or more lyrical variations making the whole flows graciously long through shifts of mood and tempo, very much in the Albert Sandler tradition. By contrast, his contemporary 'Hutch' show a much heavier and plodding percussive style dedicated solely to accompanying himself.

During a tour of Britain, once Harry became established as her accompanist, he began to move in the same circles as she did, both professionally and domestically. He met many of Gracie's family in particular Tommy her brother, who had appeared with her on stage(with his accordion-playing partner Nino Rossini) her brother-in-law Douglas (Duggie)Wakefield and would continue to do so in her early films.

---

[24]   Undated (c 1940) BBC broadcast Introduction to a programme about Gracie by conductor Louis Levy

[25]   Rex Walford 2004, *Harry Parr Davies,* Oxford Dictionary of National Biography, p. 369

[26]   Muriel Burgess with Tommy Keen, 1980, *Gracie Fields,* W H Allen, p.83

He spent time with the noted and expert talents of Herbert Farjeon and Harold Craxton.[27] Farjeon was a key figure in contemporary London theatre. He was an able lyricist, theatre critic specialising in Elizabethan drama and a revue theatre manager. He was an invaluable source to approach for help in orientating Harry to an entertainment career.

Craxton was a noted pianist, accompanist and composer. He became Professor at the Royal Academy of Music from 1919 to 1961 and taught piano at Matthay's Pianoforte School on Wimpole Street from 1919 to 1940. Earlier, he himself had earlier been a pupil there. From him Harry could learn how to accompany soloists better and how to appear as soloist. Harry was making progress in his professional career.

---

[27] BBC Radio interview with Harry interviewed by Leslie Perowne on 7 February 1940

CHAPTER 3

THE SONG-MAKER

Publishers

Very likely through the agency of Bert Aza and resultant musical link-ups of various film companies with publishing houses Harry's music came to be known to a number of well-known publishers of light music other than Lawrence Wright. These were:

- the venerable publishing firm **Chappell**, originally set up in Bond Street in 1818, but by this time with New York offices did much of publishing Harry's music;
- **Francis Day and Hunter**
- **Keith Prowse**, another popular London musical firm started in 1878 and
- and later **Sterling Music Publishing Company Ltd** of Sydney for the Australian market who published some of his songs for Gracie's film in the 1930's.

Sometime in 1934,[28] probably on the advice of some of his friends and associates, Harry had been involved in setting up (probably through investing) his own publishing company, the **Sun Music Publishing Company Limited.**[29] During its hey-day, it regularly published new songs each year. They sometimes published his music, e.g. the score and sheet music of *Dear Miss Phoebe*. Some publications were 'hits' others less so as would be expected. Whoever the company's publishers/ editors were, they from time to time showed themselves shrewd enough to pick successful songs for publication over a period of 20 years. In 1937 it was *Boo-Hoo;* in 1941 *Let me Love You To-night;* in 1947, *Chi Baba, Chi Baba,* The two big hits were in 1949 *Lavender Blue* and in 1951 *Too Young*. No doubt this gave Harry yet another source of income.

Besides songs for films and then revues and complete musicals, Harry wrote a lot of one-off songs, seemingly for specific people to sing, but others possibly just to satisfy his creative urge.

Harry must have found the backstage atmosphere of bustle and intrigue bewildering after the relatively orderly days of school and home in Neath. Nevertheless, he became involved with Gracie's professional and domestic life. More confusingly for him, he would witness her rather restless domestic scene as she drifted from Archie Pitt into the arms of artist John Flanagan and others. On the other hand, he encountered the close family networks around her a kind of substitute for his own in Neath. It was the beginning of a close working friendship with her.

His personality traits

He carried out his accompanying Gracie despite having some personality difficulties away from the keyboard. He had an utter lack of subtlety. According to Gracie, he could feel 'that road (rode?) out', (possibly meaning flat or weary) which seemed to be most of the time. He was obsessive about his bowel function. The indications are that he suffered from some kind of obsessional disorder bordering on autism. Once started on a project, he found it difficult to 'switch off', even for food. Having set

---

[28] The year of the earliest song *Believe It Beloved,* I have found so far, is in 1934. The latest date is 1951.

[29] It lasted many years and was taken over in 1970's by *Sony/ATV/EMI Publishing.*

himself goals, he could be irritable about incidental things, like the poor pianos he had to play on during their Canadian tour.

At other times, he was kindly, funny, very reliable, truthful and importantly always there. Gracie recalled *We became friends. He was as Welsh as they come, and temperamental and would often pick a row just to make himself feel better. But we had a brother-sister affection for each other and he became part of the family, who accepted him as much I did.*[30] In many ways, Harry's function was as a provider and enabler of those around him. He didn't particularly like the being the focus of attention himself, but enjoyed helping others.[31] His developing role as song-writer and accompanist to Gracie brought him further in to the 'show business' limelight. Gracie and he spent a lot of time together over the succeeding years until her operation and the outbreak of war.

During a tour of Britain, once Harry became established as her accompanist, he began of course to move in the same circles as she did, both professionally and domestically. He met many of Gracie's family in particular Tommy her brother, who had appeared with her on stage (with his accordion-playing partner Nino Rossini) her brother-in-law Douglas (Duggie) Wakefield.

His songs

What type of songs did Harry compose? Ones which reflected mainly contemporary models and which, while diverse, proved a workable structure for music aimed at performers on the concert platform, (mainly Gracie), films, (first of all Gracie of course, then George Formby and many others). Later he diversified into stage revues and musicals for the popular light music market. Where did he compose them? He remarked in one newspaper that he preferred to do this at home. His sister said he used to walk round Victoria Park Neath. Later after they moved to Swansea, he used the Gower peninsula as his place of solitude for working out his songs. What is notable throughout his output is a facility for melody welded to the words he is setting.

---

[30]   Fields, Gracie, 1960, *Sing as We Go, The Autobiography of Gracie Fields*, Frederick Mulle, p.107

[31]   Bill Hanks, 2005, *The Sweetest Song in the World*, p.9, billhanks.co.uk

He was influenced by British folk song, Welsh hymnody, British musicals, popular revues, music-hall ballads, Viennese style operettas, Eric Coates, Edward German, Gilbert and Sullivan. British revues and musicals were dominated by Noel Coward, Vivian Ellis, Ivor Novello (another Welsh composer originally with a Davies surname!), Noel Gay and Horatio Nichols. Added to the foregoing was American *Tin-Pan Alley*, contemporary crazes, like the Charleston, jazz, swing and Latin American dances.

American musicals and its film scene, familiar on both sides of the Atlantic showcased the multiple talents of George Gershwin, Jerome Kern, Irving Berlin, Cole Porter, Richard Rodgers, (responding so fruitfully to lyrics from Lorenz Hart) and ex-patriots from Hungary like Siegmund Romberg and Emmerich Kalman and Rudolf Friml from Czechoslovakia and many others. The distant reflection of these voices, their harmonic progressions and harmonies can be heard at different times in his music.

One of the best features of Harry's songs is their clearly crafted structure. There were 3 main types - a basic **song** - short introduction, a melody (often repeated twice), with a middle contrasting section then a repeat of first with a final chord or flourish.

More frequently used was the second used in his earlier days the American **Tin-Pan Alley model** with its three distinct sections - introduction, (4 bars), verse slower part about a problem or situation (16 bars) and refrain (32 bars), which was usually repeated and gave a more up-beat solution to the ideas in the verse. Harry did not use this model at all rigidly. It was more a flexible base use in response to the lyrics at hand and something to fall back on..

Lastly there is the older **strophic model** for songs, following in style either of folk song or the music-hall narrative song. They have of course still an introduction-verse-refrain structure. However, the verses are there for their narrative content and so last longer than the Tin Pan Alley model with the refrain being relegated to becoming the same tail piece after each verse. Somewhere in the song, there may be an interlude for some speech-over or an instrumental break e.g. George Formby's ukulele.

Harry uses the common major keys (or relative minor), especially B flat, C, D, E flat, F and G. Remote keys with 5 or 6 flat or sharps would put amateur (and some professional players) off. He does use G flat major (5 flats) in his later musicals. The vocal range of his published songs is normally about an octave and a half. There are two likely reasons for this. Many of the artistes had a limited vocal range (apart from Gracie and Patricia Burke). Secondly, the songs published were meant for an 'amateur' audience to buy and so had to be besides being melodious both playable and singable. Similarly he uses 4/4 or common time for musch of is usic from marches through to dance music like the charleston, the quickstep, the foxtrot, swing numbers and with Latin American flavour and for more traditional styles like music hall ballads and romantic or whimsical songs. Some numbers are deceptive. Although *Sing As We Go* feels like a 2/4 quick march, the beat is 6/8 through using double triplets. This gives it a great lift when sung. He does the same in contemporary *Joe the Jolly Marine*. Alternatively, he uses waltz time for more nostalgic or sentimental moments or even mock–continental numbers.

All this is by way of his being particularly good at fitting melodies to lyrics in a natural way. He makes key words in the verse fall at the appropriate accent in the music, sometimes dropping this in pitch to an unexpected note rather than the one used conventionally. It avoids triteness and is particularly effective n more romantic and whimsical features such as mimicking music hall and nursery rhyme models where the lyrics seem to ask for it.

His harmony is essentially diatonic. He gives support to the voice by playing by the melodic line usually in the treble with suitable harmonies and rhythm. At the end of many phrases where the voice is sustaining a note, he places counter short melodic phrases under the voice. Occasionally does he use dissonance, e.g. in passing phrases or at the end of introductions where it resolves when the voices enter.

He stated in a newspaper interview that he liked Debussy, Delius and Wagner. Their influence is more apparent in the shifting, often chromatic harmonies he uses in chords under the melody to create uncertainty of mood. (He played Debussy's *Clair de Lune* as a popular concert solo).

All this is background preparation to support his skill at fitting melodies to lyrics in a natural way. He makes key words in the verse fall at the appropriate accent in the music, sometimes dropping them in pitch to an unexpected note rather than what would be used conventionally. This avoids triteness and is particularly effective in more romantic and whimsical features such as mimicking music hall and nursery rhyme models where the lyrics seem to ask for it.

Adjusting to the performer

The vocal range and cadences within the song are normally carefully tuned to the artist featuring them and partly dependant on the rhythm and/or mood of the verse. Gracie was often given phrases which explore her middle and upper register. She also often did this on her own initiative finishing a song with an upper cadence or flourish from the basic tune ending on a top B or C. Other artists had to transpose such apparently simple tuneful songs as *Sing as we go* in order to sing them comfortably.

For George Formby, who was obviously more limited in range and timbre than Gracie, Harry keeps the melody simple and clear tuned to his vocal range but providing passages for him to do his famous ukulele improvisations. The songs themselves have many felicitous touches in harmony and melodic counter-phrases. He did the same for other singers as time went on..

Orchestration

Where it comes to orchestrating his music, there is no clear evidence how or if he did this. His prior training with Parrott and Walford Davies are likely to have provided him some elements of how to do this exacting task. Nevertheless he followed contemporary practice and left arranging the orchestration and how the piece would be finally heard to the musical director of whatever film, play, revue or musical he was involved at the time. The arranger would add orchestral colours to the harmonised melodies Harry provided, extend or curtail the structure as appropriate, sometimes eliminate the introduction, put in bridge pieces or ritornellos as needed. The resultant work had significant differences in detail when published as sheet music from what is heard in films or sound recordings.

In practice, conductor/arrangers were an essential contributor to the feeling of film, but rather kept in the background. They were hard working, qualified musicians of experience in both stage and film work but not in the public eye as the stars were. Nor were they acknowledged usually by the 'serious' music fraternity. For most of the films with which Harry was involved during the 1930's, Ernest Irving was Associated Talking Picture's (ATP) main residential conductor/arranger. Others like Bretton Byrd, Charles Williams and later Debroys Somers performed this task for some of Harry's revues and musicals. A case in point, there is a MSS version in Neath Library of the first page of the overture to *Lisbon Story* – presumably Harry's thoughts about it. The printed score is quite different.

Lyricists

From early childhood as has been already noted, Harry wrote his own words to his music, a habit of a lifetime. He had some facility in versifying and wedding word and music easily. His early songs for inserting Gracie's film were therefore all his own. Harry's word setting is exemplary, clearly based not only on the varying metre of the lyric, itself based on speech patterns of the English language, sometimes quite colloquial in their diction but with appropriate emphases. This results in a coherent feel to the song.

Besides his own lyrics, he set a quantity of verse by other people. This was sometimes for a single song, sometimes for a single project such as a film or revue. However from about 1936, he began to work with specific writers. These would become his main source of lyrics, although not totally exclusively. While all are fit for purpose, like his own verse, they lack the adroitness of Cole Porter, Lorenz Hart and Irving Berlin or Noel Coward.

In succession, the main providers of lyrics for Harry (apart from himself) were:

Eddie Pola. From 1935 to 1940 he provided a few workmanlike lyrics for solo songs.

Roma Beaumont From 1936-44 she was a singer in some of Ivor Novello's shows providing some pleasant if slightly sentimental lyrics.

Roma Campbell-Hunter From 1938 to 1940, she provided a number of lyrics. She can turn out quite attractive slightly whimsical items.

Phil Park From 1939 to 1945, he was a consistent partner of Harry's for films, revues and individual numbers. Although he can sometimes provide ideas for Harry to respond to, his verse can be rather predictable in meter and conventional in sentiment, (as seen so often in his many translations of operettas by Johann Strauss, Lehar and Offenbach for amateur performances).

Barbara Gordon and Basil Thomas From 1942 to 1950's they continued to provide Harry with variety of ideas and metres but sadly also wrote the rather dismal lyrics for *The Knight was Bold.*

Harold Purcell From 1943 to 1950. Harry and he collaborated regularly. He provided Harry with a consistent quality of words to set. His diction and metre are similar to that used by Christopher Hassall for Ivor Novello's musicals, namely romantic, mildly witty and above all fluent. Harry responded quite consistently to what Purcell provided for him.

Christopher Hassall From 1950-55, this accomplished BBC broadcaster provided the lyrics for *Dear Miss Phoebe* and some later songs. They were working on new material with him up to the time of Harry's death.

There were a number of one-off collaborations through the years. (see lAppendix 2l List of Chronological Works)

To some extent, by reading between the musical and lyrical lines, an attempt to understand Harry's emotional responses to the external events in his life can be made. The topics of many of his songs reveal concerns. Love is the most frequent, whether expectant of fulfilment, a partly idealised statement of feeling, frequently nostalgic, mentioning sleeplessness and dreams like *Counting Sheep* and *Lying Awake and Dreaming.* but never erotic. Once working more independently of Gracie, many songs take on a more underlying nostalgia, including songs and pieces about Capri.

Many numbers, especially in the early days sing about seeing sunshine in things. This allowed him to accentuate the bubbly side of Gracie's personality with whistling songs like *Just a Happy Little Tune*. Other songs were frankly sentimental, e.g. the one written jointly for their mothers, *Mary Rose* Harry provides it with a nostalgia with an almost Donizettian turn of phrase. Linked with these, weather references include the hackneyed rainbow, blue birds and rain followed by better weather occur as trite symbols of lovers and their plight.

Places figure less in his songs. There are songs with an Irish flavour (*Valley of Dreams)*, a Scottish flavour (*Glen Echo)* a London scene and one or two titles with an Italian provenance including *My Capri Serenade* and *Anna from Anacapresi.* He provides Gracie with more developed numbers as in his effective, but mild spoof Viennese waltz, *Do You Remember My First Love Song,* with its upward extension to A.

There is no evidence Harry spoke Welsh, nor did he have a distinct south Walian accent. His recorded voice (like his sister 'Billie') shows a clearly articulated voice, mostly BBC Kensington in sound, except occasionally a slight Gallic lilt detectable in a few words. Despite the fine Welsh tradition of vocal music, it was not a directly significant contributory influence on his output. Even in *Jenny Jones,* the music published tends to remains more West End than *Cymru.*

For the time being his developing role as song-writer and accompanist to Gracie carried him with her further into 'show business'.

CHAPTER 4

GRACIE'S FILMS (1932-4)

Many British films were made at Ealing Studios and Harry increasingly provided songs for them. The relatively new 'talkie' medium had drawn players from many British music hall and revues. The latter had remained popular in London and often toured provincial theatres throughout Britain, despite the increasingly well-made 'silent' films. They continued to be popular during the 1930's, getting another boost at the beginning of World War Two (WW2). The war they would provide Harry with a new vehicle for his talents.

Gracie's films after her first film *Sally in Our Alley* in 1931 began to include members of her family as they were already known from her time on the variety stage. In particular, there was her brother Tommy Fields, her sister Edith Fields (Edie) and Edie's husband Douglas (Duggie) Wakefield and other members of Gracie's previous entourage. They now appeared regularly her films, *recruited from music hall, variety, musical comedy and the radio. The majority of those from the halls shared roots with and*

maintained the allegiance of their predominantly working class following.[32]
The range of talent was wide. It included character actors, speciality acts,
experienced artists of all ages and rising young players like Kenneth More
and Muriel Pavlov.

Loose plots were devised to provide more or less convincing reasons
for set solos, comedy sketches, balletic and acrobatic routines, previously
seen in revues. Sets were often stagey. On the other hand, there are also
undertones, especially in the earlier films, of social justice being played
out through Gracie as its main agent. For some reason, in many of them
Gracie seldom 'gets' her leading man (especially <u>not</u> handsome suave John
Loder). She usually uses comic means to obtain social justice. Indeed, in
two of Priestley's scripts (*Sing As We Go* and *The Show Goes On*) despite
the buffoonery, a message of social equality emerges. To make it seem more
authentic, actual documentary footage is used.

Orchestrally those film scores made in Ealing Studios were well served.
The London Philharmonic Orchestra, opportunely founded in 1932 by Sir
Thomas Beecham, was the studios' resident orchestra. Later others like the
Queen's Hall Light Orchestra or noted brass bands like Bess o' th' Barns
were used. They played the soundtracks, usually conducted by Ernest
Irving, Brendan Byrd or Charles Williams experienced composer–arrangers
in their own right. While they provided playing of quality, only gradually
did the actual quality of sound improve. Similarly, the integration of studio
set and the addition of more documentary footage became smoother.

Looking on the Bright Side This, the next ATP film for Gracie was shot
at Ealing Studios and released in September 1932. It had Graham Cutts
as very able director and Basil Dean as co-director, screen writer (the story
line was his own idea) and producer. Musical arrangements for this score
were made by conductor/pianist Carol Gibbons.

The plot is simple, possibly an idealised even prophetic reflection of Gracie's
her relationship with Harry. Gracie and Laurie (Richard Dollman) are cast
as lovers, who have joined to form a duo, in which she sings and he writes the
songs. When Laurie gets a taste of fame, he runs off with a glamorous actress

---

[32]   Robert Murphy (editor), 2009 -3rd Edition, *the British Cinema Book,* p.
      107 - Richard Dacre, *Traditions of British Comedy*

but he returns to her again for the sake of the act. Harry's song *I Hate You* was indeed used in the film, where it is given two hearings, the second by Gracie. Its expressively plaintive tune in a bluesy style has strange bitter but evocative words. Its intensity make it the best musical number in the film, despite it not being acknowledged in the film list of attributions.

Harry as part of 'Gracie's professional entourage participated in three other branches which promoted her career. Gramophone recordings had now improved their quality with the development of the electrical over the earlier acoustic. This resulted in Harry being recorded playing his piano accompanying Gracie either on his own or as part of an orchestral backing. Added to this they made a number of BBC broadcasts together for both national and local radio stations over the next years.

This Harry's next film venture for Gracie shows he had come to learn what was effective for Gracie's personality and for her remarkably even soprano voice. She often embellished the song with her own brand of decoration leading to a climactic finish. Harry must have seen *Sally in Our Alley* which presented him with a paradigm for his own songs for her.

Domesticity

About this time, Gracie used the money she had accrued to buy houses. She acquired a villa 'Il Postino' on Capri, which she developed as 'La Canzone del Mare'– Song of the Sea'.[1]

She bought 'Greentrees', 19 Finchley Road, Hampstead which she refurbished as her latest London house and Harry stayed there frequently; she remarked later *we had a brother and sister affection for each other and he became part of the family, who accepted him as much as I did.*[33]

She bought two houses in Peacehaven near Brighton Sussex for her parents the second at 29 Telscombe Way as they preferred a sea view. The first had been 'Telford' 17 Dorothy Avenue North. This became the Gracie Fields Children's Home and Orphanage at Peacehaven in Sussex. The Theatrical Ladies Guild started in 1891 as an association

[33] Fields, Gracie, 1960, *Sing as We Go, The Autobiography of Gracie Fields,* Frederick Mulle, p. 109

looking after theatre folk. It was looking for a place for children of those in entertainment in the widest sense. when their parents could not look after them, because of their commitments at home or abroad.. They included children of actors, singers, dancers, travelling circus people and so on. In response to an approach from the Guild's secretary Lottie Albert in 1933, Gracie donated the house to the *Guild.*, The official opening ceremony was attended an assortment of guests - American character actor, Charles Coburn, witty Liverpool comedian Rob Wilton, comic singer/pianist Norman Long, comic actor, Charles Austin, charity promoter, Sir Harry Preston and Labour politician, John Henry Thomas among others. Gracie continued to finance it, although she left the Guild the responsibility of running it.[34] She often visited it and mingled with the children, even doing a Christmas concert with Harry and an unnamed Santa Claus.

Harry had some obsessional traits, for instance absorbed in playing the piano most of the day, he would complain that he didn't get any breakfast, despite Mary Barrett and Gracie's mother continuing leaving him trays.[35] Harry often accompanied Gracie to Capri, especially to prepare for their next film. He also took up smoking, a habit he continued for the rest of his life, as many photos show. This is likely to have affected his health in later life.

He told in a later interview how they worked together *Before making a film Miss Fields and I usually manage to escape to Canzone del Mare (Song of the Sea), her beautiful villa in Capri.... I 'fiddle about' at the piano for a couple of hours, after breakfast, developing ideas and carrying out experiments. When I get a good theme I ask Miss Field's opinion. If she likes it I go ahead and work it out. Together we discuss ideas for lyrics and possible situations for the numbers.... She is most particular that her audience shall understand every single word she sings.... and.... avoid distortion of diction.*[36] [37]

---

[34]   The Official Gracie Fields website graciefields.org

[35]   *Sing as We Go, The Autobiography of Gracie Fields, 1960,* Frederick Muller p. 108

[36]   *Song Writing for Gracie Fields,* unsourced undated (c.1936)USA newspaper interview with Harry in Parr-Davies Collection

[37]   There s a draft by Gracie for the song which Harry developed in the above collection.

Gracie and Harry playing cards on Capri

This Week of Grace This film released on 14 September 1933 was made in Twickenham Studios, directed by Maurice Elvey after a dispute with Radio Pictures (RKO). (The title strongly echoes that of Noel Coward's successful play *This Year of Grace*. With a fee of £20,000, Gracie features in a film intended to show some equality between the social classes. It has good sets and costumes. Thomas Percival Montague Mackay was the conductor and music arranger. The songs were published by Francis, Day and Hunter.

The story unfolds about Mr and Mrs Milroy (Frank Pettingell and Minnie Raynor) a well-matched pair cinematically and their two children Joe (Duggie Wakefield) and Grace (Gracie). Father and son run a garage in a haphazard way and rely to some extent on Gracie's wages.

Grace loses her job in a factory when she is late. She gets a job eventually after meeting the eccentric Duchess of Swinford (Nina Boucicault) in the park. Grace is to be housekeeper at the duchess's home, nearby Swinford Castle. She wants Gracie to sort out a group of scroungers, who are reducing the family estate to poverty. The situation is complicated by her family coming to live. Initially kept at a distance by the other staff, librarian (John Stewart) helps Grace to become more socially adept. The result is she soon captivates them through her personality and hard work and falls in love with the Duchess' nephew, Viscount Clive Swinford (Harry Kendall). Henot only rejects his current girlfriend for Gracie, but proposes to her. Later she wrongly believes that he has married her thinking she was rich. She leaves him at the altar to go and take a job back home on the stage working in the chorus line. Eventually the misunderstandings are cleared up and the couple make up. Harry provided 5 well-crafted songs each showing up different aspects for Gracie's vocal art:-

> *A Melody at Dawn* with words jointly by Gracie and Harry. This has a pastoral wistful feel being a more meditative song that the others in the score. The first verse has many open air references, the second is more about dreams. The refrain mingles these sentiments to an underlying tango rhythm until the final chord - a delightful number.

> *Happy Ending* with words also by Harry has a Tin Pan Alley structure. The 2 verses denote the present state, The refrain an effective expression of hope for the future.

> *Mary Rose* has words jointly by both Gracie and Harry. The structure is like that of *Happy Ending* but instead is a slow waltz. The 2 verses have slow lilting phrases slowing for the refrain. This has an early romantic somewhat Italian feeling. This makes the tribute to both Harry's and Gracie's mothers a wistfully charming song.

> *My Lucky Day* has words again jointly by Gracie and Harry. He however modifies the usual *Tin Pan Alley* with 2 verses and a refrain. This contrast makes the song sound glad and feeling alive at the present.

Lastly *When Cupid Calls* has words by Harry. This is a pleasant perky rather girlish number, with usual structure, which Gracie vocalises appropriately.

For the film, orchestration were done by the experienced conductors/ arrangers Thomas Percival and Montague Mackey. The variety, effectiveness and freshness of these songs went some ways to making Harry's music for *This Week of Grace* popular enough to be recorded by Edison Bell Winner Records Company, who specialised in recording middle-of-the- road pieces from the popular to light classical. He had also acquired a place for himself (this address is on a draft of *Just a Catchy Little Tune* for the next film) - 168b Sutherland Avenue, Maida Vale W 9 – a convenient pied-à-terre for Central London. This was a basement flat in a brick built terrace. He would return to the area after he was 'demobbed'.

Sing As We Go This next ATP with Gracie film directed by Basil Dean and released in September 1934 is a lively, entertaining comedy with a message of uplift, shot mainly in a quasi-documentary way in Blackpool using local people in the location shots. It was fortunate in a number of ways. Its screen play was written by John Boynton (JB) Priestley, who is particularly remembered for his 'reality–orientated' novels *The Good Companions* (1929) and *Angel Pavement* (1930). Its scenario editor was Australian-born Gordon Wellesley, who had just started to write for British films and would spend the next 30 years writing for both British cinema and TV. The film reinforced the growing popularity of Gracie as a film star.

The whole film works as a happy mixture of humour and sentimentality and also gives a social portrait of not only the hardship but the stoic humour of working class life in 1934. The main storyline is about Gracie Platts (Gracie), a Lancashire mill-girl working at Rochdale's Grey Beck Cotton Mill, living at home in a house full of broken clocks with Uncle Murgatroyd and shrewish Aunt Alice. She also loves her boss at the factory (John Loder) but from afar. Gracie loses her job caused by a strike. *Even t'clocks are on strike,* she comments. Undeterred, wearing shorts and bearing pots and pans, she cycles to Blackpool to find a job, asking a policeman (Stanley Holloway) the way and dithers, nearly colliding with a tram. Arriving among the holiday crowds at Blackpool, she has a go at a variety of jobs, chambermaid, fortune teller, song demonstrator, magician's assistant, toffee seller, contestant in a beauty competition, even a human spider chased around site and falling into the *Tower Circus* water tank at part of its finale of the *Circus*. All these situations show her going through a repertory of comic and romantic 'turns' and songs.

The strike ends, her boss goes off with the winner of a beauty contest (Dorothy Hyson). Whereupon Gracie leads the mill-girls back into the now reopened Grey Beck Mill with the marching song *Sing As We Go,* accompanied by the brass band Besses o' the Barn from Bury. The film also had a sterling supporting cast including 13 year old Muriel Pavlow.

Harry's title song was the final spur to ensure the film's popularity. It remains one the songs by which he is still remembered and foreshadowed future success as a composer, Now reworked for Gracie Fields from unused *Peter the Pup*, it is basically a quick march akin to a schottische with a bugle call which Gracie vocalised in the repeat. The conductor arranger for this and most of the films with Harry's music during the 1930's was resident musician Ernest Irving. The title song in particular was a cheery song for the difficult days of the Depression and Irving orchestrates *Sing as We Go* in number of guises until it becomes almost a *leitmotif* expressing Gracie's determination to succeed. The other two songs Harry wrote for the film were:-

> *Just a Catchy Little Tune* is well suited to Gracie's jaunty music hall style, which include phrases to show her whistling ability. She sings it in Blackpool Tower Theatre and Harry lengthens the usual *Tin Pan Alley* structure to make the song an effective and effervescent song of happiness.

> *If all the World were Mine,* alternatively is more meditative and longing in the vein and structure of a song like *Happy Ending* in *This Week of Grace* and provides a contrast to the other 2 songs. Harry is showing his versatility for Gracie's benefit.

Harry and Gracie at 'Greentrees'

They spent a lot of time together over the succeeding years until her operation her re-marriage and the outbreak of war caused them to be apart. He now became more and more quite at home at Gracie's houses, very much as a younger brother particularly at Greentrees or at her parent's house at Peacehaven. He needed the time and space not only to work at learning new repertory for Gracie but to compose new music for her films or concerts as well as making up different songs just to please himself. His other place of quiet was to go back home to Neath. He had by now left the Maida Vale flat to become resident with Gracie as his address is given as Greentrees.[38]

Harry later recalled how he was involved with Gracie's songs ending up on screen, *When making a film she concentrates on the sound part first of all usually doing as most of the big recording jobs on Sundays. The song is then 'played back' on to the floor, where Miss Fields, with the camera focussed on her, supplies the visual part of the number. Together we map out the routine*

---

[38] This is the address e.g. on 'banknote' Christmas card of 1937 and on 30 November 1938 boat passenger list

of a number about three weeks before the actual recording. It is difficult work, as the final arrangements take days to complete, and often the music needs additions even after the last days of 'shooting.[39]

It is likely Harry was somewhat in love with Gracie, even if it was platonic. Many of his solo songs are concerned about gaining or being in love or nostalgia for unobtainable lost love. Gracie intent on her own marital and relationship problems possibly did not (or did not want) to recognise that he had romantic feelings for her. Their relationship though close for many years, remained professional and friendly.

Love, Life and Laughter The film released in March 1934 is similar to Sigmund Romberg's *Student Prince* and Franz Lehar's *Die Csarewitch* namely the love of prince and commoner denied as a vehicle for Gracie, but Harry did not provide any music for it.

However, he wrote three songs during the year.

> *Croon to Me* recorded by Leslie (Hutch) Hutchinson - a sentimental song which falls easily in Hutch's range and *The Night You Sang 'O Sole Mio'.* Finally there ia a little gem possibly written at Harold Craxton's suggestion for Walter Widdop the distinguished operatic tenor, *Tree Top Lullaby*. In a simple format reminiscent of Arthur Butterworth's *Shepherd Cradle song* and of other English composers in a pastoral mode it is a charming almost artless song, particularly good at exploiting the *mezza voce* middle register of the tenor voice. It is possible that Harry love of Wagner lead him to hear Widdop at Covent Garden as Siegmund (in 1932 *Die Walküre*) or as Tristan (1933 *Tristan und Isolde*). Widdop sang in oratorios and concerts, where he could have wanted a suitably quiet song as a contrast to more weighty items.

---

[39]   Unsourced undated (c. 1936) USA newspaper interview vide supra

CHAPTER 5

GEORGE FORMBY AND
S. AFRICA (1935-7)

Monty Banks

A new man had entered into Gracie's life, Mario Bianchi (his name anglicised as Monty Banks). This was brought about through Bert Aza, her agent, who had business with him and brought him to Greentrees.[40] This meeting would mark a new departure in the film-making business for both Gracie and for Harry. Gracie moved on to work with Monty as film director displacing Basil Dean, who began to turn to other stars. Harry continued to write for Gracie, but also began to write music for others which Basil Dean and Monty were promoting. Domestically, things for Harry continued as before, with Monty another person who came to know Harry and use his talents.

---

[40]   *Sing as We Go, The Autobiography of Gracie Fields,* 1960, Frederick Muller p. 91

After working on 4 films for Gracie, Harry during 1935, embarked on working with another film star, the Northern comedian, George Formby. Monty was the director of the first 2 films. Harry gave George both sentimental and comic songs in 5 films from 1935-44. George's humour was more slapstick, his musical style more robustly comic but like Gracie, it derived from the music hall. His singing while less accomplished in tonal quality than Gracie's was very witty and accurate. He usually topped his songs off with an interlude of virtuoso performance on the banjolele. Harry's contribution to George's repertoire was small but fitted George's requirements whether comic or sentimental very ably

No Limit Monty had had a long acting career in American silent films. When the 'talkies' he moved in to directing. He now became involved with the British films often appearing in cameo roles. moving into George Formby films. George came to enjoyed Harry's company and they spent time in the pub. Possibly Beryl, George's wife, thought him a more suitable companion for George[41] rather than George ogling the ladies.

A chimney sweep from Wigan George Shuttleworth (George) dreams of winning the Isle of Man TT Race. With money 'borrowed' from his grandfather Shuttleworth (Edward Rigby), George builds the "Shuttleworth Snap" motorcycle after failing to join the *Rainbow Motor-Cycle* team. He not only succeeds in winning the race but getting the girl Florrie Dibney (Florence Desmond) as well. Of the 4 songs in the film. Harry wrote one *Your Way is My Way*. The ever present Ernest Irving served as the film's musical director and arranger.

Move to Swansea

Harry came home for a dinner given on13 July in his father's honour as singer and honorary secretary of the Neath Male Philharmonic Society at the Cambrian otel, Neath. The Society's President, Herbert Waring presented them with a combination bureau-book-case and hall chair. He thanked David John for his work as secretary to the society over the last 9 years, especially his arranging for the recent visit of Paul Robeson to sing

---

[41] Bret, David, 1995, *The Real Gracie Fields,* J R Books Ltd p.76-7 He includes offensive personal comments about Harry made by Monty and Beryl Formby. They may be possibly be true but are not given any source.

at a recent concert. He wished them well in their new home in Swansea. Harry's father responded that he would always take an interest in the Society. Under the conductorship of a Madame Wynne Richard-Thomas, LRAM, a musical programme was given including popular songs by Harry.[42]

Harry's mother and father moved from Neath to 9 Lôn Cadog, Cwmgwyn, Swansea. It was a larger dwelling in a more up-market setting, when compared to the terrace house in Neath. It had double bay windows, small gardens front and back, set in a more spacious street lay-out. Being above Swansea Bay it had clear views towards Mumbles Head and the Islands. Glennys worked at the *Midland Bank* on Windsor Street in Swansea. 'Billie' worked at Lloyds Bank on Wind Street, where she met her future husband. She married 28 year old Geoffrey David in Autumn 1936 and they lived at nearby Lôn Draenen, Sketty, Swansea.

Look Up and Laugh This next ATP film was directed by Monty Banks and was released on 4 August 1935. It had a script with a social message with again written by J B Priestley and his Australian-born scenario coordinator Gordon Wellesley. A vehicle for Gracie, it is less socially perceptive or believably realistic than Priestley's earlier film script. Its sets are more studio bound with the effect of the whole being more like a stage farce especially in the long 'demolition' scene in the department store. It provided supporting roles for members of the cast who ha came from silent and talking film and the stage or were new talent like Kenneth More.

Grace Pearson (Gracie) returns to Plumborough for a holiday after touring in a revue - *Mind Those Legs.* There is trouble at the old market where her father is a stallholder in the old market and she learns this is to close completely and be torn down. She therefore embarks on a battle to save it from intended closure by Belfer with the agreement of the bumbling mayor (Rob Wilton) and his cronies on the local council. They are opening a more modern emporium. Inits place. The long established silent film and talkies character actor Alfred Drayton plays Belfer a rich tycoon. A young emerging actress Vivien Leigh plays his daughter. (She got a fee of £300

---

for this bit part).[43] Grace's brother Sydney is played by her brother Tommy Fields and brother in law Douglas 'Duggie' Wakefield plays Joe Chirk a friend. In true farcical style, Grace set about making Belfer the tycoon totally uncomfortable in the opening of his new store.

She helps children wreck the displays in his store and then attacks the owner in a social context in a special 'prima donna' scene. Having locked an Italian singer due to appear as a guest for the opening in a closet, Grace takes her place and presents the kind of comedy in which she excelled. Harry has a cameo role, appearing in morning suit and tie as the accompanist to Gracie (together with a clarinettist). She sends up operatic foibles using Violetta's double arias at the end of Act I of Verdi's La Traviata, *Ah! Fors è Lui* with its cabaletta *Sempre Libera* as a basis. Singing a text in garbled Italian and French (e.g 'amour' for 'amor') sings it more or less straight, but the cabaletta – in reality a fast waltz, she musically garbles interjecting all kinds of warbling, but ending up with a clear high C. What a pity she did not record it straight! Harry as her accompanist supports her not only by his musical accompaniment, but with facial expressions and comedy timing.

She suffers a setback when Grace's brother falls for the tycoon's daughter, who is talked round. The store is blown up by a convenient gas leak, leaving the market to continue as it was founded originally by Royal Charter (cf *Passport to Pimlico*). All ends well though Gracie is faded out rather than having a sung exit. So she has been successful. The songs by Harry were:

> There is a bright-and-breezy song to a quickstep tempo, *Look Up and Laugh*. After slower verses (2 of them) there is a refrain of up-lifting good humour Gracie supplied Harry with the verses, which are partly used. It shows clearly how they interacted to arrive at the completed song,[44]
>
> *Anna from Anacapresi* (Horatio Nichols again provided some of the lyrics) is a 5 verse nonsense waltz song about nationalities which

---

[43] Darwin Porter and Ray Moreley, 2011, *Damn You, Scarlett O'Hara – The Private Lives of Vivien Leigh and Laurence Olivier*, Blood Moon Productions, p. 192/3

[44] [H] Parr-Davies collection.

Gracie, Tommy her brother and Duggie her brother-in-law take up. Each one has a verse about a person from a different country, Gracie has a verse for the Italian of the title, Tommy and Duggie, verses about the Spanish Alfonso, the Swiss Hiwitch and the Welsh Tony from Tonypandy with Gracie ending with Russian Olga. After the introduction, each verse has a comic rigmarole revealing the character assumed with the voices come together in a concerted number before the next verse. It is a well-crafted 'music hall' number for a group of seasoned entertainers.

Lastly frankly sentimental but optimistic, *Love is Everywhere* is a simply expressed song of the joy of being in love, the refrain being particularly haunting. Again these three songs showed his versatility in reflecting the situation in the film.

Away from film, Harry wrote other songs to different authors and in different styles, again possibly for consumption by USA as well as British markets. The title *Bring Back the Girl in the Old-fashioned Gown* sounds like a nostalgic reprise of 1919 hit song *My Sweet Little Alice Blue Gown* and *Carnival in Spain* similar to any Latin American number of the time.

The oddest piece of music that Harry wrote for Gracie was *'Erbert 'Enery 'Epplethwaite.* This is basically a comic verse monologue about a Lancashire lad wanting to be a crooner. The verses are underpinned with sustained chords in the orchestra as Gracie declaims in the same way as Stanley Holloway did with his popular of the time monologues about *Sam* and *Albert.*

Joe the Jolly Marine is similar in feel and structure to *Sing as We Go* in its infectious '3 naval step' rhythm - a quick march tempo. In keeping with its theme, its prevailing mood is akin to *There's Something about a Soldier* song in the 1934 cartoon short *Betty Boop.*

Blue Bird of Happiness is unique in Harry's output, in that he provided the lyrics (not the music) with experienced lyricist Edward Hayman for a haunting tune tenor by Hungarian ex-patriot classical composer Sandor Haymati. This was for Jewish cantor/operatic for Jan Peerce who made it his signature tune.

Harry was possibly fulfilling reciprocal part of his contact, by providing further lyrics for the song for the British part of the market just as his songs were published in USA. Peerce's version for RCA Victor is a singular charmless version being much too operatically full voiced and further spoiled by a central sentimental *parlando* section to it. Others recorded it - Shirley Temple, Gracie herself, Jimmy Durante. Jo Stafford and Gordon Mc Rae recorded it giving it a due gentleness and calm appropriate to the music, which no others reach. Gracie finally closed her relationship with John Flanagan the artist, but not before he had done a fine an oil painting of Harry for his 21st birthday.[45]

South Africa

After this, Gracie, Tommy Fields, his comedy partner Nino Rossini, Monty and Harry sailed on 21 November for Cape Town for a South African tour on the Union Castle line steamer, *Windsor Castle* a four funnelled steamer built in 1915 but soon to be refitted.

While on board ship, Gracie accompanied by Harry gave a concert. Once they had disembarked in Cape Town, Gracie was given a lively street parade reception. Her first concert there was with an orchestra, but it was only for half-an-hour. For many other concerts, Harry played for her. She said about him that the tour would never have been such a success without the brilliance of my pianist. While she here praised Harry's abilities, she also recalled how touchy he could be. There was another Welshman, a conductor in Care Town. He and Harry both got into their heads that the other was mimicking his Welsh accent with very intense non-verbal results. This incident showed how touchy Harry could be and how easy it was for Gracie and Harry to fall out.[46]

The tour took them on to Johannesburg and surrounding towns like Benoni. Notwithstanding the busy schedule, they had time for sightseeing.

---

[45] It is now hangs in Neath Library

[46] *Sing as We Go, The Autobiography of Gracie Fields, 1960,* Frederick Muller p. 106

They went off on 7 January in the New Year 1936 and visited East Geduld gold mine near Springs, dressed in suitable mining suits and helmets, Cullinan diamond mine near Pretoria and a snake farm[47] with aquarium, aviaries museum and tea-rooms. The tour was so wildly successful that they extended their stay by a further 6 weeks. At the final concert, Gracie typically sang Harry's song, *You've Got to Smile When You Say Goodbye.*

They all sailed home from Cape Town on Thursday 26 March on the Union Castle line's *Stirling Castle.* They gave a typical variety concert on board on the Cabin Class Deck. Harry gets two spots, first as the 'warm-up' act and then accompanies Gracie as 'top-of-the bill':-

1   *Harry at the piano played a selection*

2   *Doreen – xylophone*

3   *Jack Daly – the Irish Entertainer [a pleasant baritone who specialised in Irish songs]*

4   *Raymond Smith –Ventriloquist*

5   *Tommy Fields and Nich Rossini – A Kouple of Komics*

Call out of Prize Winners

6   *Impressions – Disa Bolton*

7   *Payne and Holland - in Burlesque Episode*

8   *Freddie Phyllis and Anne – the latest in Rhythm. [modern dance act]*

9   *GRACIE FIELDS*

On 25 May safely returned they broadcast from the BBC to Australia. These broadcasts had started in 1932. Even before she went to the southern hemisphere Grace was known and appreciated there. Broadcasting from

---

[47]   Possibly the *National Zoological Gardens* of Pretoria dating from 1898. It today houses all mentioned above.

BBC was an important way of communicating to the Empire what was happening in UK.

Keep Your Seats Please This was the second ATP film that Monty directed as a vehicle for George Formby. It was released 1 August 1936. George Withers (George Formby) is set to inherit jewels from his Aunt Georgina (May Whitty). Deceived by unscrupulous lawyer, (Alastair Sims in good form), whom he seeks to help. It transpires that they are hidden in 1 of 6 antique chairs, but which one? Before he can get to the auction, they are sold off separately and so he has to find them.

> Harry wrote one song, *Binkie's Lullaby* for the little girl Binkie, who appears in the film (although possibly not used) to lyrics by Arthur Wilson. Again the music was conducted and arranged by Ernest Irving.

Queen of Hearts This film was yet another ATP film, released on 5 October 1936 had Basil Dean as Director and Monty Banks as producer. In it, Gracie and Monty both used and reflected the time they had spent in South Africa. Its script was by Clifford Grey and HF Maltby. The cast apart from Gracie included Monty (in cameo as passerby), her sister Edith Fields, John Loder (as Derek Cooper) and stage-singing actress Enid Stamp-Taylor (Yvonne).

Harry in cameo role in 'Queen of Hearts'

Harry appears in a cameo role complete with cigarette as street busker and unemployed miner in an outdoor café in London has a hand written notice 'Wife and Three Kids to Support'. Grace Perkins (Gracie Fields) an ordinary working class seamstress is mistaken for a rich patron of the art by a show's producer. When she's asked to back a new show she plays along with the charade, hoping that she can become the production's leading lady. She auditions and finds herself in the show, where instead of singing she dances the apache dance with dancer Carl Balliol.

When the show finally opens in the final scene set in Venice, she emerges from a gondola and starts to sing a spoof Viennese operetta waltz song with words by Harry, *Do You Remember My First Love Song?* a slow waltz admirably suited to Gracie's range and style. She fully meets the challenges in the song which stretches through 2 octaves.

Another song featured earlier in the picture, *Why Did I Have to Meet You* is reminiscent of *I Hate You* in its characteristic slightly sour nostalgic mood. The lyrics are by Clifford Gray who provided some of the other lyrics used in the film. It is a sophisticated number, its melody and its harmonies giving an unsettling feeling with a middle section, termed an interlude recalling the past. In the recording of the song, Gracie having repeated the first section with vocal tracery leaves the tune in the air with a high climactic G. These two numbers reveal more ambitious and less conventional musical planning from Harry They are also more demanding on the singer, vocally and emotionally.

Harry wrote a Christmas number possibly intended for a Gracie Christmas concert or just the popular Christmas sheet music market. It had slightly odd lyrics by Roma Campbell-Hunter, *the Angel* (or *Fairy*) *on the Christmas Tree*. Girls want to be angels in USA (or in UK fairies) on the Christmas tree, while boys are just happy with presents they receive. The message of the lyrics, without taking them too seriously is a slightly esoteric one about the superiority of female aspirations. This song has a *Treetop Lullaby* structure, a lightly scored introduction. It still occurs in Christmas popular song anthologies.

Harry also received the unheard-of advance cheque of £1000 from Horatio Nicholl to write songs for his publishing firm in the future - a reward indeed for his original persistence! Harry had set occasionally some lyrics by other writers but had not yet found a consistent co-worker. Roma provided him lyrics for some of his songs from this time on, either as single items or for British revues.

Outside Dr Nagaeli's Klinik in St. Moritz

Gracie, her parents and Harry went off to ski resort St Moritz for a winter holiday. They were photographed wrapped up warmly in a sleigh outside a clinic. The hoarding announces a Doctor Naegeli, a doctor and women's doctor with an X-ray facility. Was this merely an uncanny prognostication of things to come for Gracie, or had she come for a private consultation?

Chapter 6

USA TOUR (1937)

❖

There was a request for Gracie to open the new cinema in Gateshead, the Black's Regal High Street and she responded by going there after the St Moritz holiday and opening it on 5 February. Albert Black was the promoter of this chain of cinemas. He was the brother of George an impresario for whom. Harry would work regularly during WW2.[48]

Using the media

By 1937 Harry's reputation both as pianist and as a songwriter for Gracie's and George Formby's light comedy musical films was well established. His songs were sung increasingly not only in films, but in concerts, broadcasts and on records. Gracie herself from 1932 sang and recorded his songs as did many other artistes. The BBC Western Programme broadcast on 17 March 1937 for instance was a selection of Harry's music arranged by Leonard Morris and Garfield Philipps and played by Garfield Philipps.

---

[48]   Evening Chronicle

The Show Goes On This ATP film released in April 1937 was the last film for Gracie directed by Basil Dean. It included some autobiographical material drawn from Gracie's life, i.e. a rag–to-riches formula. Sally Lee (Gracie) has a mother (Amy Veness) and father (Edmund Rigby). She works at the mill and loves Mack McDonald (John Stuart). Plucked from the mill by a composer Martin Fraser (Owen Nares) who needs a voice capable of performing his songs, she comes to love him also. She hits the big time with more popular material while he fades away from TB.

> Gracie sings *Smile When You Say Goodbye* from the deck of the *Queen* Mary to a group of sailors. This is one of Harry's most enduring songs set to his own words. Hee is said to have composed words and music in 30 mins.[49] It anticipates many similar songs during the war years. With the familiar Tin Pan Alley structure, it is a slow foxtrot, which after introduction, questions in the verse, the refrain gives an answer in the title.

> Other songs Harry wrote for film were, *A Song In My Heart, My Love For You,* (lyrics by Eddie Pola) *Success Cockalorum, The Show Goes On,* (lyrics by Harry) and *We're All Good Pals Together.* (lyrics by Haines and Harper, who gave the words and music to so many of George Formby's songs).

> This last song is a jolly sea-side chorus again written for duo Flanagan and Allan, very much a quick march., the verse singing of welcome and camaraderie and the refrain has lots of lively oom-pah sound accompaniment making it a pleasantly rowdy number. Haines and Harper provide Harry not only with a standard version of their lyrics, but give 3 alternatives - Cockney, Dude and Scotch (sic).

Ernest Irving as usual arranged the film score.

Before its actual release, Harry had already sailed on 5 March 1937 from Southampton to New York on *Queen Mary* (the London address on

---

Red Letter Days, *The Gracie I Know* c. Mid-September 1955 interview with Harry, the ship's manifest is 31 Finchley Road).[50] He wrote home in a spirit of youthful wonder the next day with letter headed paper:-

> *Cunard White Star*
> *R.M.S. Queen Mary*
> *Wed. 6.*

Dear All,

> *Thanks for cards. Gracie received hers also and sends her thanks. We set off this afternoon at 2 p.m. It is a wonderful ship. You should see my room. I even have an electric fire in it, also my own bathroom and lav. It really is marvellous. It's like an enormous hotel.*
>
> *We set out back on April 15th from Hollywood. So we shall get back in London ten day later. No more news, Love Boy.*

Once they have travelled down to California they got off the train at Pasadena, the station before Los Angeles to avoid the media.

Pasadena with Gracie signing autographs

---

[50]   David Bret, 2010, *The Real Gracie Fields The Authorised Biography*, JR Books Ltd. p. 67

A photo shows them getting into the cab, with Gracie signing autographs, Harry looking on. The cab would take them on to the Beverly Wilshire Hotel, Beverly Hills. Harry writes home again in a state of wonderment:

Monday March 15ᵗʰ

Dear Glenys,

> *We arrived here at noon after a very tiring three days in the train[51]. This is really a wonderful place. I went to Twentieth Century Fox studios this afternoon. They have a wonderful place.*

> *We have a flat in this hotel, which is <u>the</u> hotel in California. Marlene Dietrich has only just moved out of this flat & underneath us we have Clark Gable. Also Myrnna Loy is statin on third floor. We are on the 7ᵗʰ floor. It is a lovely flat with drawing room, dining room, kitchen, hall etc. We are looking right over Hollywood.*

> *I think I shall be lucky and get a song in the first film. Of course, the competition is terrific. She is going to do a few broadcasts. The first will be with Eddie Cantor. She is going to sing "Smile when you say goodbye" & she is going to make it in this country her signature tune, like Sally in England. Chappells of New York have bought the rights from Lawrence Wright & are putting it out in this country very soon. I fixed it before I left New York. I shall get very little money out of it because naturally Lawrence Wright purchased the American rights. Still I shall get Performing rights. Apart from that if it is a hit, it will*

---

[51] The train was the *Atcheson, Topeka and Santa Fe Railroad's* express 'The Super Chief', which ran from Chicago to Los Angeles in 39 hours 49 minutes. Nicknamed *The Train of the Stars,* it was a diesel powered streamlined all-Pullman sleeper with dining room and a bar/lounge. To make a connection with New York, the party would have travelled on luxury sleeper steam hauled expresses such as New York Central's *'20ᵗʰ Century Limited'* or rival Pennyylvania Railroad's *'Broadway Limited'*. Each took at this time 16 hours and 30 minutes for the journey. Total travel time therefore was 56 hours 15 minutes as a minimum, without adding station transfer time in Chicago.

do me good. The studio[52] are giving G. a big lunch tomorrow and the next day a big party to meet all the stars. No more news, Boy

P.S. Has Daddy started his new job yet?

If you can write to this address up until April 15th we stay here for the complete tour.

The lunch mentioned above must have beeb painful for Grqacie as she had had a total clearance of her teeth and had new dentures put in immediately. The fare was roast beef, Yorkshire pudding and roast potatoes!

By the next Sunday, Harry is savouring the different personalities he has met and their gossip, looking how Gracie comes over, as well as having some musical and financial ambitions himself:- *Sunday (22nd)*

Dear All,

Just another note. We went to Charlie Chaplin's to dinner. He was marvellous. I got on very well with him. He is very musical. He is the most charming person I have <u>ever</u> met. So cultured and a perfect host. Paulette Godard was there.[53] She was delightful. Also Constance Collier. She is <u>the</u> woman out here. She is English society & coaches the stars. – She coached Norma Shearer for Romeo and Juliet & Garbo for Christina. We are going to her house to dinner tomorrow night. King Vidor a big director was there also. Gracie sang and they were charmed. Then Chaplin did some funny songs. They were marvellous. Do you remember the tune in "Modern Times"? well I happened to say I liked it and he was thrilled so he told me if I wanted to write a song on it I could do as I liked. So I shall trun it into a popular song. It is a great publicity angle. Tell Daddy he can put it in the Post if he likes that I am writing a song with Charlie Chaplin.[54] We are going out with them again on Thursday.

---

[52] Presumably 20th Century Fox

[53] Charlie's second wife

[54] The request reported in some newspapers by Chaplin for Harry to write for Hollywood could have been made at this time

Dinner with Charlie Chaplin, Grace, Monty and Harry

Last night we went to a dinner given to G. by the Lancashire people of California and after we went to the Clover Club.[55] Robert Montgomery, Miriam Hopkins[56], Binnie Barnes[57] etc. Graie is quite a society success out here. They go for the English here. Tonight we have been to the Trocacadero[58] where all the big people dine. And when I was dancing with her, I could see all the people discussing her. She looks exceptionally smart and her teeth have made a tremendous difference. Gracie Allen and Burns (you know Burns and Allen) have invited us to dinner next Tuesday. Gracie has the reputation of being a terrific snob because she wouldn't go out to all the parties she had been asked to. She couldn't because was having her teeth out. She only goes out with the people. Chaplin is considered it out here. Miriam Hopkins told Binnie Barnes that she thought G. was 'too society' to both with then and very catty because G. wouldn't lunch

---

55   On *Sunset Boulevard*, i.e.at 8477 Sunset Strip a noted and notorious gambling casino and night club, raided eventually by police and closed in 1938.

56   Versatile American actress

57   English supporting actress, domiciled at this time in USA

58   Another fashionable night club on the Strip

with her. After all if she accepted every invitation she'd go daft. We are broadcasting next Sunday with Eddie Cantor.

I shall be very sorry to leave here.

I must buy a camera and take some snaps.

No more news

Boy

The proposed broadcast on *Eddie Cantor Texaco Show* on 29th did not happen. Eddie Cantor invited Gracie Monty and Harry to dinner to prime her about the show. He in a rather bumptious way tried to tell Gracie how she needed to remodel her act change to fit in what he perceived was the way things were done in USA. This progressively unnerved Gracie so much, her mind went blank. *Harry jumped up "what 'll you sing, Grace?"* She could only thing of *Sally.* She sang it far too loudly because she was nervous. *Harry was thudding away at the accompaniment, his eyes and mouth screwed up in an agonised expression.* Despite Monty and Harry continuing to smooth things over, they left. Gracie didn't do the radio broadcast.

Harry also met Shirley Temple and *the late George Gershwin, who, after playing his own dance numbers specially composed for the next Fred Astaire film,*[59] *invited his judgement.* The trio spent Christmas and New Year at a ranch near Palm Springs, tasting barbecue food and enjoying the parties held.[60]

They returned to Britain no doubt for the Coronation of King George VI which was to take place on 12 May. Shortly after this they made an appearance in an early telecast variety programme called 'Star', televised from Alexandra Palace on 22 May 1937. They appeared with BBC Television Orchestra conducted by violinist composer Hyam Greenbaum. It shows Gracie and Harry willing to respond to the new technology,

---

[59]   RKO's "Shall we Dance?"

[60]   Fields, Gracie, 1960, *Sing as We Go, The Autobiography of Gracie Fields,* Frederick Mulle, p.116-8

undergoing the preparation and by facing the cameras and equipment of TV in 1937.

As they commonly did throughout the years, Harry's family came to see what ever he was involved with. For instance Rosina Harry's mother came to London during the third week in July. Mother and son went to see Gracie's latest film *The Show Goes On* (and hear the latest 6 songs from Harry in it of course). Rosina also saw him accompanying Gracie at the Palladium on 19 July. He is reported to be going in mid-August to Capri to work with Gracie on her next film, *We're Going to be Rich,* prior to the filming starting in September.[61]

---

[61]   South Wales News, 27 July 1937

CHAPTER 7

A BUSY 15 MONTHS (1937-1938)

This was the beginning of a busy 15 months of composition from this time onward until Christmas 1938. These were the next steps for Harry slowly to emerge as his own man.

For the end of 1937, he penned another Christmas number, *Let's Have an Old-fashioned Christmas*. His ability to give a personal message in a humorous and original twist was shown when he also sent his friends an imitation banknote as a Christmas card. Its address was still Gracie's house Green Trees, 31 Finchley Road, St. John's Wood, London NW8. Harry crossed the Atlantic to New York at the end of 1937 - this time by plane with Gracie, Monty Banks and Mary Barrett, her companion/secretary. They travelled to Palm Springs and Hollywood. There he bought himself a loud sports jacket and a pair of pale green trousers. He said, *Movietone City I love it.*[62] They returned in January, for Gracie to receive the CBE for her charity work and services to entertainment from King George VI in February 1938 at Buckingham Palace, this together with distinguished concert pianist Harriet Cohen.

---

[62]   Muriel Burgess with Tommy Keen, 1980, *Gracie Fields,* W H Allen, p.84

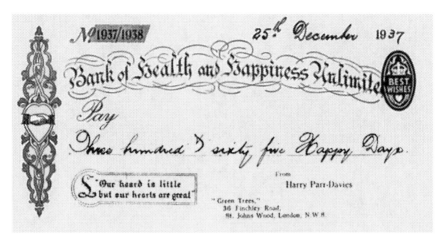

Harry's Christmas Fun Cheque

In 1938 besides his usual accompaniment of Gracie on stage, on records and in broadcasts, he provided 15 songs. For films, there were 2 for two Gracie, the same for George Formby. However, he also wrote for two newer talents, in some ways similar to Gracie, there were 2 numbers for 28 year-old singer/dancer Marjorie Browne in a Carol Reed film and 3 for the film featuring 18-year old singing actress Betty Driver for Basil Dean.

I See Ice This was the next ATP film featuring George Formby and Harry wrote 2 songs for it. Its well-worn plot has a naïve fellow outwitting criminals, more sophisticated than him. This theme went on to be recycled with variations for later British comedians like Norman Wisdom and Morecambe and Wise as vehicles for their essentially music hall humour on the big screen. George Formby in this film, directed by Anthony Kimmins released on 10 February 1938 is the usual main inept comic character in the guise of a 'prop' manager for an ice-ballet company.

This provides some background spectacle as well as love interest through Kay Walsh. George somehow invents a camera concealed in a bow-tie. Unwittingly he snaps crooks in suspicious circumstances. He has to do something to prevent them and gets caught up various comic adventures. Harry wrote two songs for the film: *Noughts and Crosses* and *In My Little Snapshot Album.*

Noughts and Crosses is a slow swing number which Harry employs for George in slightly skittish romantically bashful mood, while he plays the actual game on the restaurant table cloth to woo Kay Walsh. Starting with a bouncy figure, Harry sets Roma Campbell-Hunters verse with phases of apology, which rise in pitch as he assets himself. The refrain starts with a jerky rhythm to give it a querky swinging feeling to the lyrics concerning George's self-depreciation. This is followed by a smoother tune about the game, but finishing the insistent rhythms of the introduction. Unusually the refrain while musically the same repeats with a new set of words of similar sentiments to the first. In the recording George consistently sings 'Oughts' instead of 'Noughts'! Nevertheless in this music, mood voice and patter come together with great charm.

The situation is the same for *In My Little Snapshot Album* with the heroine sitting beside George in the film and reacting as best she can, the verse has a number of *double-entendres*.[63] It is in fact a classic music hall ballad in a very quick march tempo with a short refrain to the words of the title, at the end of each of four verses, explaining how he came to get a camera and the effects of using it! In the film and recording, there is a ukelele episode. It makes a neat song well tailored for George's talents.

Another song *Mother1 Mother! What a Naughty Boy am I* was published in 1938, but was not included in that year's films. With George's usual lyricists (Harper and Haines),it verse reads like an alternative to *Mother What'll I Do Now*, written by George Formby and Fred E Cliffe in the prison scene of the film. Using some of the refrain and an introduction in march time, the refrain has 'Mother' repeated 8 times before it gets going. Harry ends it with a perfunctory phrase, repeated a tone higher. It has a further 3 verses. The whole is a suggestive patter song for George to perform in his own inimitable fashion. It could well have fallen foul of the Lord Chamberlain and British Board of Censors and so was replaced by the other song.

---

[63] Bret, David, 1999, George Formby, Robson Books Ltd. p 71 The song had verses by Haines and Harper. Bret without referring to any source comments that Harry had offered it to Gracie, she said it would be better for George as it was too rude for her!

We're Going To Be Rich Gracie's films were by now regarded as popular money-spinners at least in Britain. In this new picture, backed by American dollars from *20ᵗʰ Century Fox*, she made a bid for more universal appeal, the production company aimed at something different. It reflected in some ways the time Gracie and Harry had spent on tour in South Africa and the visit to the Johannesburg gold mine the previous year. Two British born actors, now Hollywood stalwarts, Victor McLaglen and Brian Donlevy were Gracie's male counterparts and the young Coral Browne completed the quartet.

Directed this time by Monty Banks, the musical arranging was given to experienced conductor/arranger Irishman Bretton Byrd. This film was set in Victorian times with suitable costumes to match the two settings - Australia and South Africa. Kitty Dobson, the *Lancashire Lark* (Gracie) is a singer well loved by Australian settlers. She is married to ne'er-do-well Dobby (Victor McLaglen). He is too fond of alcohol. She is giving a final performance before returning to England. She sings the attractive waltz song *The Sweetest Song in the World.*

> This song has a gentle theme in the verses (2 of them) putting nostalgic statements, ending in mild triumph. The refrain is confident in its expression of love, making a charmingly sentimental song, very suited to Gracie's softer style.

Dobby tricks her into going to South Africa. He has bought half-shares in a loss-making gold mine there. Once there, after a brawl, Dobby lands in gaol with Monty in a cameo as another prisoner. She decides to make money by singing to the 'trekkers' in a saloon, owned by fiery-tempered Yankee Gordon (Brian Dunleavy). She has to fight him off. His erstwhile ex- saloon singer/lover Pearl (Coral Browne) retaliates by trying to make up to Dobby. He dumps him in a horse trough, but Gracie tells him that they are finished. Gordon and Dobby fight. Dobby loses the contest, and Pearl floors Gordon with a frying pan! Gordon now acts as a marital peacemaker and Kitty and Dobby make it up.

Its success encouraged 20ᵗʰ Century Fox to make a further offer of a £20000 contract for 4 more films. Harry only contributed 2 songs to this film.

The *Trek Song* arranged from 2 Afrikaans tunes *Vat jou goed en trek Fereira*, and *Sarie Marais*. Harry starts with a music-box-like sound to introduce it. In the first song he supports the tune with a accented drone-like beat. Immediately the smoother second tune follows with 2 strong march-like beats to accompany it. The first tune is repeated and a coda using the music box sound again. The version Gracie recorded has the verses, which Harry writes in English sung by a male voice chorus, while Gracie sings the original words in very passable Afrikaans. It makes a very attractive number in either format.

Lassie from Lancashire John Paddy Carstairs later the director of Norman Wisdom comedy films) promoted a light comedy musical in the British National Productions film *Lassie from Lancashire*. Dance band leader and studio musical director Ronnie Munro arranged the music. It featured the pretty 28 year old singer dancer Marjorie Browne. Released in August, its naive plot seems to cash in on the popularity of Gracie and a northern venue. It reads like a cross between *Look on the Bright Side* and *the Show Goes On* with Marjorie Browne in a what could be a typical Gracie role. The story written by Ernest Dudley, in collaboration with Doris Montgomery from her original, involves Jenny (Marjorie Browne), a struggling young actress who joins her Dad (Mark Daly) when he moves into his sister's boarding house (Elsie Wagstaffe). She tries to work the pair to death. Jenny however begins to fall in love with Tom (Hal Thompson), a struggling songwriter. The two become close but their romance is nearly ended when the star in a local pantomime jealously plots to destroy their love. Jenny and Tom overcome the star's attempts to part them. They dream of a positive future after being offered a theatre contract in London's West End. Like Gracie Marjorie was a Lancashire girl and had played a number of singing and comic roles on stage and in films. Harry supplied 2 songs to his own wordswhich lie well in the mid-voice.

For the First time in My Life I'm in Love is a romantically lilting waltz and *Good Night, Little Sweetheart*. This is a gentle lover's farewell song – even a kind of lullaby. The verse describes sunset and the refrain is smoothly soothing ending.

On 23 August a more social occasion took place. Gracie was asked to a beauty contest held in the afternoon at the Royal Ordnance[64][65] sports and gala ground at Euxton, west of Chorley. Sir John Jackson, Deputy Lord Lieutenant of Lancashire was one of the judges. In the evening there was an at home - reception held at Prospect House Whin Lane, Wheelton near Chorley to celebrate Sir John's 70th birthday. Besides Sir John, Lady Jackson and their daughter Pat, there were a number of guests including Gracie Harry and the *Cafe Colette Orchestra*, a small spa-style orchestra conducted by Walford Hayden (his wife had been invited too). Sadly, Sir John died a month later.

Penny Paradise In her autobiography, Betty Driver remembers the ATP film *Penny Paradise* as the last Basil Dean made for Ealing Studios. His time would be taken up with the organisation of ENSA during the war. Released on 24 September and written by Thomas Browne, Walter Needham and Thomas Thompson, it was directed by another co-writer Carol Reed, later famous for his film, *The Third Man*. After launching the screen careers of Gracie Fields and George Formby, Dean wanted to create one more 'star'. He chose Betty - an eighteen year old. He offered her a 5-year film deal. Looking like a young Gracie, she had a pleasant voice and had previously appeared as both music-hall singer and in London revues.[66]

The film opens with some action shots of Liverpool harbour. It is about a Liverpool tugboat skipper, Joe Higgins (Edmund Gwenn, who had top billing in this film, later becoming famous in films as Lassie's master). He thinks he has won the football pools. He gives his job up and starts to celebrate his win by throwing a party for family and friends in the local pub. Some of these hope to get hold of a share of the winnings. He pays particular attention to a widow Clegg (Maire O'Neill) whom he fancies. His daughter Betty (Betty Driver) is propositioned by a rogue who thinks there is a chance of some money. The party stops altogether, when Pat (Jimmy O'Dea), Higgins' Irish first mate on the tugboat has to admit that he forgot to post the winning coupon. Betty sorts out the problems

---

[64]   Where the 'Bouncing' bomb would later be made

[65]   Lancashre Evening Post, 22 August 1938

[66]   Betty went on to become a long term favorite bar maid Betty Turpin in TV series *Coronation Street*

of the elusive fortune and her own romantic mistakes at the same time. It closes with Higgins coming out even better than he hoped. His former employer offers him the captaincy of the best tugboat on the Mersey, a job he had always hoped to have.

While O'Dea's song is clearly provided for comic effect, Betty gets 3 songs by Harry to his own lyrics (with Gracie like titles and content) *Learn How to Sing a Love Song., Stick Out Your Chin* for Betty, a light hearted number and *You Can't Have Your Cake.* Ernest Irving and Gideon Fagan shared the music arranging for the film.

On 10 November, Harry and Gracie with orchestral backing recorded Adams well-loved song *The Holy City* and the song *Biggest Aspidistra in the World* for *Regal* Zonophone.

It's in the Air This is usually thought to be the best and funniest of Formby's films, directed by Anthony Kimmins for ATP. It was released in November and was intended as a morale booster. for the nation. Despite Neville Chamberlain's return from Munich in the days with his message 'Peace for our times' on 30 September, there was an inevitable feeling that war was going to happen. This feeling is partly captured in this film, where George Brown (George Formby), rejected by the Home Guard wants to join the Royal Air Force (RAF). A friend of his leaves behind some very important documents, whereupon George realises his dream of joining up could soon come true. He puts on a RAF uniform and delivers the documents, mistaken for a dispatch driver from head office (HQ). He sings a mocking song about the Sergeant Major (SM) (Julien Mitchell), who retaliates by making the butt of his jokes. This means he stays at the air base. George falls in love with the SM's daughter Peggy (Polly Ward). When he realises who George actually is, he threatens to report him. On the annual inspection day, George attempts to flee ending up inside a plane. With the inspector looking on, George's solo air plane display is memorable as he is the only passenger in a pilotless plane as it does 'loop-the-loops'. George manages to land the plane and is as a result accepted as a flyer by the RAF. The SM actually insists he should be commended as he wants to cover the mistakes that have been made.

Harry wrote one airy number, *It's in the Air*. George sings it to Peggy. The verse conveys George's anticipation of change accompanied by a brisk quick march in the refrain. It is a deft combination of march and romance with room for George's banjolele solo on the refrain's repeat. The words and music of this were by Harry. The song was later adopted by RAF and other forces as a WW2 battle song.

Keep Smiling This was the next 20th Century Fox with Gracie (as Gracie Grey) and was directed by Monty Banks, released in December. The cast included the wire haired terrier Asta, Tommy Fields (as one of 3 Bolas), comedian M'sieu Eddie Gray (Silvo), Roger Livesey (Bert Wattle) and Nino Rossini (another of 3 Bolas). Basically it is a revue cast as a series of turns in a road movie. After the company are cheated out of money by an ex-manager, a group of performers club together to buy a bus and travel around the country doing shows. Again Harry contributed 2 songs set to his own texts:

> *Giddy Up* is a charming pantomime-like character song about the old horse Susan as the company go home from the fair. Harry sets it at a steady plod, the verse telling about the old horse 'Susan', the refrain encouraging her to take the company home.

> *Swing Your Way to Happiness* is a moderate quickstep to classic *Tin Pan Alley* formula. Harry provides a cheery upbeat number to his own words. The refrain incorporates many jazz intervals and harmonies to give it an underlying feeling of tension which is eventually resolved - a very satisfying genre piece.

Harry and Gracie also broadcast on. *BBC Northern Programme* (441 metres) 10 pm the BBC Variety Orchestra under Larry Ross, Gracie sang with Harry at piano.

Other work as an alternative outlet to stage and film work for Gracie and Harry were radio broadcasts from the commercial radio station, *Radio Luxembourg*, the sole radio broadcast alternative in Britain to the BBC. He wrote one of his most effectively nostalgic songs (verses jointly written with long time publisher friend, 'Horatio Nicholls' and Roma Beaumont *London is Saying Good Night*'. It was used to close down the station.

Basically a fox-trot, marked 'slowly', it begins with high pitched chords in the accompaniment suggesting London bells.. The refrain resembles a lullaby as night descends on the city and awaits the dawn. Harry uses short chromatic figures in the accompaniment. The whole makes it one of Harry's most satisfying songs.

Other songs he wrote were *The Sweetest Girl in the World* and one which had some popularity at the time, *The Sweetest Sweetheart of All,* with words by Welsh-Greek musician songwriter. Jimmy Messini who proceeded to record it. It was then featured by duo Herman and Constance on a broadcast from Central Pier Blackpool and also played by Joe Kirkham and his band. Reminiscent in sentiment but less beguiling than the earlier *Mary Rose* thes song comments about ageing motherhood. The tune is repeated in a second verse recalling the love for the old lady.

This marked a busy year with Harry beginning to widen his scope; 1939 would see him widen it even further.

CHAPTER 8

TIME FOR CHANGE (1939-1940)

1939 was a not a year of unmitigated happiness, indeed it would bring major changes to the world as well as to Gracie and Harry. They made another recording 17 February for Regal Zonophone featuring *Umbrella Man*. Also early in the year, preparations for what would the last film of Gracie's for which Harry worked on musically were in hand.

Shipyard Sally Its script was by Karl Tunberg, Don Ettlinger and its director was by Monty Banks for 20th Century Fox in the early part of 1939. It was a typical Gracie film with a social message of uplift for the workers. The plot shows how the years after the Depression have affected working people i.e. little money, poor morale. After footage showing activity on Clydeside, it shows an uncle (Sydney Howard) and niece (Gracie) a couple of failing music hall artists. Using her own money, Uncle buys a pub for her for the benefit of unemployed Clydeside shipyard workers. Gracie heads off to London to challenge the attitude of politicians and the shipyard owners. Her Uncle keeps on bungling things, but she always rallies. She allows herself to be mistaken for an American singer/dancer, Linda Brown at a well-to-do reception. She performs a jazzy number *I Got the Jitterbugs*, after that a Latin American vocal dance medley of dances written by Harry *In Pernambuco*, (indeed Gracie learnt the rumba for this section of the film). The result is the building and launching of a new liner. A cue for Gracie to sing *Wish Me Luck as You Wave Me Goodbye*. The film was released a month after war was declared on 20 October and it became with Vera Lynn's wartime songs one of the nation's war anthems.

> The song has words by Phil Park, who often supplied lyrics for Harry's work at this time. Harry keeps all the introduction and verse to a minimum as if hurrying to the uplifting and tantalising memorable refrain. This a brisk swinging march constantly surging upward, faster and more determined than the verse. After a brief contrasting section, it ends triumphantly. It seemed to sum up all that would happen in the immediate future and how people should face it.

For the rest of the year Gracie was enveloped by financial physical, emotional and marital difficulties. They were to have an effect on Harry as well as everyone else around her. First of all Harry's accustomed London refuge with Gracie's household at 'Greentrees' disappeared, when Gracie sold it to pay for accumulated unpaid income tax at the end of May.[67] Having felt unwell during the film shoot of *Shipyard Sally* Gracie had a biopsy. This showed cervical cancer. She underwent surgery to remove this as well as a hysterectomy as part of the treatment in 14 June 1939 at the Chelsea Hospital for Women. Nearing 40, it meant farewell to her having any thought of having children in the future. During the necessary convalescence, she typically made another record with Harry on 30 July singing Paul Rubens *I Love the Moon*.

More important for her future happiness, the application for her divorce from Archie was presented on 22 July 22 and after a few days she went off to Capri for some private time with Monty. As a likely affectionate salute to Gracie while away, Harry wrote unusually for him a purely piano (or orchestral) piece, *September in Capri, an Italian Picture*.

---

[67]   Fields, Gracie, 1960, *Sing as We Go, The Autobiography of Gracie Fields*, Frederick Mulle, p. 99

In fact for Harry the time he had spent so close to Gracie now ended. Her interests and future choices allowed him to emerge as a performer and composer in his own right. While Gracie was convalescing he started and continued to writing music for 2 revues for George Black. He gave his address in the West End as *Grosvenor House Hotel*. This was a Hotel with a large ballroom where resident band leader Sydney Lipton and his Grosvenor House Band from c. 1931 to 1967 played. Dating from that time is a song, *The Pretty Little Quaker Girl*. by Harry to words by Roma Campbell-Hunter, Harry's regular lyricist at the time. It was recorded by 15 year old singer Celia Lipton, Sydney Lipton's daughter. She was hailed this side of the Atlantic as the 'British Judyl Garland'.

> The naive sentiments expressed in this song were very much of an innocent age about falling in love. The verse questions how Quaker youths meets. A reply is received in the refrain of how a couple communicates, meets and weds. Harry provides a simple almost child-like gently flowing tune perhaps owing something to Lionel Monkton's popular musical *The Quaker Girl*.

Second World War

At the beginning of the Second World War i.e from 3 September 1939 onwards, all London theatres closed as a sign of the national emergency. It was an unpopular move. A change in the Government's official attitude meant that by Christmas entertainment came to be seen as an essential morale booster. So, theatres in London and the provinces once again opened their doors.

George Black was a British theatrical impresario who controlled many entertainment venues during the 1930s. Born in Birmingham, he as a young man helped his father set up some of the first permanent cinemas in Britain. By 1928, he had taken over the management of *General Theatre Corporation*, a chain of theatres, cinemas and dance halls headed up the Corporation most important theatres, the *London Palladium* and *Hippodrome*. He rebuilt the latter in 1937. Both these theatres under Black during the next few years would play a significant development in Harry's life as a composer.

In 1931 Black organised *Crazy Week* there, gathering acts together which later grew into the *Crazy Gang*. He continued to promote shows and revues for them at the Palladium until his death. Many theatre programs of the 1930s had the words *Produced by George Black* on their cover. He presided over the merger of GTC with *Moss Empires* in 1932. This put him in control of a new company *Moss Empires Group* with a chain of 53 theatres. In 1937 and 1938, he directed two films; *The Penny Pool* and *Calling All Crooks*.

Harry now moved from being an effective writer of songs either for Gracie or films to writing for theatrical revues with the more sustained musical efforts required to compose musical sequences of different moods and tempos, suitable for a variety of characters in different situations, all in the one show. After his death in London in 1945, Val Parnell as will be seen, who had been his booking manager, took over the running of the Group.

Revues had remained fairly popular throughout the 1930's and underwent a renewal during the war years, largely due to George Black promoting them as a superior variety concert with definite themes and popular artists from stage films and the vital communication link BBC Radio. Noel Coward summarised very graphically putting a review together; *Writing for a revue is a difficult delicate art as is directing a revue..... A sketch for a revue ust be quick, sharp, funny (or sentimental) and to the point with a really goo exit line. The finale of the first half would already have been agreed upon, but all the numbers had to build, and build to the number before the finale and that numbr whatever it was had to be sure-free. The second number of the second half was, still is, and always will be, terribly important. It has to be strong, or so funny, or so spectacular or whatever that the audience ...... will be comfortably in their seats, happy in the knowledge that the second half is going to be even ore brilliant than the first.*[68]

Harry as one of the song-providers had to provide these highlights. His was a comparatively sudden appearance on the revue scene at the end of 1939 writing the music for 2 West End revues. This provided him with

---

[68] Noel Coward, p. vii in Raymond Mander and Joe Mitchenson, 1971, *Revue – a story in pictures* Peter Davies

the opportunity of moving away from the more formulaic patterns of British popular music scene. He came to write solo songs of a more flexible structure, often with engaging melodies created with specific voices in mind. Responding to war-time feeling, his songs are often sentimental and nostalgic, at other times taking a quirky or comic turn. He was in preparation for dealing with the more extended requirements, which musicals would make of him from 1942 0nwards.

Black Velvet This revue subtitled *George Black's Intimate Rag.* was in 2 acts covering 18 scenes. It opened in 14 November 1939 at the *London Hippodrome*. The show's roster included Vic Oliver as a roving Master of Ceremonies, vocal impressionist Afrique, Teddy Brown (a 5' 2", 26-stone virtuoso xylophone player!), Pat Kirkwood, Roma Beaumont and Carol Lynne as the lead female beauties, the South African duo- Max and Harry Nesbitt and versatile bit-part actor, Cyril Smith. Black encouraged Harry to do the music. As usual, during 1941 it went on tour, being for instance at Nottingham Empire Theatre for 21 August.

> *Bubble Bubble* (lyrics by Roma Hunter-Campbell) was the introductory number sung by Patricia Heywood.

> Harry substituted *How Beautiful You are,* more sentimentally sophisticated when sung by rising star, Patricia Heywood. for the Shirley Temple song by Cole Porter, *My Heart Belongs to Daddy* which he disliked on the out-of-town preview in Brighton. This number is an expressive song (in E flat major to a slow fox-trot tempo). Its use of a repeated dissonance anticipates David Raksin's *Laura.* Harry simplifies the structure to an introduction and a long languorous melody. This ends with a coda extending a figure already heard in the introduction.

Later programmes reverted to the Porter song when out on post-London tour – cf. 2 week run beginning 20 May 1940 at Empire Theatre Newcastle.

> The final number, written by lyricist of *Run Rabbit Run* and *Hey Little Hen*, Ralph Butler gave a comic song *Crash! Bang! I want to go Home* to start 'celebrating' the blackout to verses verging on the farcical. It is basically a quick march with 2 strong beats in

the bar. There are 3 refrains telling of the singers predicament (the rhythm is similar to Noel Gay's 1932 success *The Sun has Got His Hat On,* (also with lyrics by Butler), interrupted by strong beats to march the initial words. Harry contributed a sung dance scene called *3 Shades of Blue* and more not attributed music for other scenes.

Debroy Somers and his Orchestra played the music and he also arranged it. The blackout song with which closed the show *Crash, Bang, I Want to Go Home.* (lyrics by Ralph Butler) became a particularly topical hit. The show ran for 620 performances and it put Harry among the popular musical elite of the day. As the curtain fell on the first night Black called his young composer to the front of the footlights telling the audience, *Here is a young man you'll hear a lot of in the future.* Perhaps the mantle of being only Gracie's pianist and composer was beginning to be cast off.

Haw Haw Black's next wartime review was to be *Haw Haw,* which opened on 22 December 1939 at *Holborn Empire.* He wanted something loud, cheerful and *risqué* and above all he wanted was the very popular comedian Max Miller as chief crowd puller. Max Miller did a variety of character scenes. He burlesqued the treasonous William Joyce, (nicknamed Lord Haw Haw) who broadcast Nazi propaganda on the German overseas radio service and so became a figure of derisive fun nationally especially to radio listeners. Max followed this up with his own version of Hitler. Then he acted as an old soldier, who had once slept in Anne Boleyn's bed and yet another soldier in the army trenches. Interestingly later Max Miller said that taking part in scripted sketches was not his cup of tea, preferring the stand-up gags he plundered from his blue joke book!

Added to all this was Bebe Daniels and Ben Lyon more lively entertainment featuring can-can dancers and tuneful songs which the public could take away with them. Haryy wrote 4 songs for the show. As *'Round and 'Round We Go, Ho-dle-ay Start the Day Right, It's Wonderful* and *Your Company's Requested* This latter song in particular shows Harry at his peak. Phil Park's words sound mildly hallucinatory. After a calm verse the refrain is in a kind of schottische tempo, desiring and imagining the lover's presence. It emerges as a quirkily effective cabaret number.

The show opened in December at the *Holborn Empire* and proved, despite its provocative title a great variety favourite of the time and it stayed at the Holborn Empire.

> Harry wrote words and music for this another waltz song which Gracie recorded, *Love Never Grows Old*. It is a gently flowing waltz, reminiscent of Romberg's *When I Grow to Old to Dream* giving a slightly faltering nostalgic effect to the words of reminiscence. The refrain follows the same kind of flowing tune with a strong 1st beat typical of 1930's waltzes.

American actors, husband and wife team, Ben Lyon and Bebe Daniels both with Hollywood experience behind them decided to stay in Britain on the outbreak of war. They were a popular couple, who played in the radio feature *Hi Gang.*

> He wrote them a pleasant folksy nonsense number during 1939 *The Little Swiss Whistling Song* set to his own words. Like *A Catchy Little Tune for Gracie* and the later *Pedro the Fisherman,* it incorporates phrases for the singers to whistle. The Lyons do this well in their recording of the song. *The* introduction taken from the beginning of the refrain, is placed an octave higher to contrast with the ump-pah sound in the bass and mimicking the higher wind instruments in a pseudo-Swiss accompaniment. The verse has phrases telling why whistling is overtaking yodelling. The refrain launches into a strict time number, with cadences to whistle instead of yodelling. The middle section is in more varied time, before the repeat and snappy ending. The pair took part in the 1941 revue, *Gangway.*

During the later part of the year, Gracie was still convalescing from aggressive surgery and Harry was in the middle of composing for his revues. He was required to register for the draft, in other words was 'called up'. Harry was to join the Irish Guards, where training for new recruits was to be held on Coulsdon Common, near Caterham, Surrey.[69]

At the beginning of the war Basil Dean the film director, together with spirited comic actor and producer Leslie Henson had founded the Entertainment National Service Association (ENSA) with its headquarters at Drury Lane Theatre. ENSA's object was to keep up the morale by inviting artistes of all types - comedians, popular singers, classical musicians - to travel out to whereever the forces were, either at home or abroad. Many entertainer s responded, including George Formby, Arthur Askey, Vera Lynn and of course Gracie. Despite what should have her further convalescence she was asked by Basil Dean to go to entertain the forces out in France. Harry was of course in the process of being called up. She baulked at performing without Harry, so she put pressure on the military and he was deferred a year.[70]

The pair thus came back together This reunion was compounded by further recordings for *Regal Zonophone* on 17 November., The programme was typical, Gracie sang to Harry's accompaniment *Wish Me Luck*, *Walter, Walter, When I Grow too Old, Old Violin*.

They set off with Monty and Marry Barrett, Gracie's companion for France. Staying overnight in Folkestone before crossing the Channel they arrived in North France south of Dunkirk. *It was bitterly cold and as we drove along the French roads, the car getting stuck in the mud and slush.*[71] When their vehicle broke down on the way, to the delight of troops already there Gracie stopped to give impromptu concert near Lens. On Christmas, Day 1939, they gave a concert for RAF in Rheims Opera House, a large theatre with imposing late Victorian front, but art deco interior. This concert was broadcast by BBC.

Gracie (and presumably Harry) returned to UK on 5 January as Harry travels to Bristol to plays solo in a Henry Hall variety concert at *Colston*

---

[69] There is no archived record of Harry enlisting in the Irish Guards

[70] BBC Interview with 'Billie' David, 1990

[71] Fields, Gracie, 1960, *Sing as We Go, The Autobiography of Gracie Fields,* Frederick Mulle, p. 138-9

Hall on 2 February. Others guest performers were musical comedy actress Sonnie Hale, crooner Donald Peers, radio singer Diana Clare.

At 12.30 pm, 7 February, Harry gave a BBC Home Service interview to Leslie Perowne, BBC Head of Light Music.[72] He describes Harry at this time as being tall dark and Welsh, with horn-rimmed glasses and a cigarette in his mouth. During the interview Harry talked about the influences on his development in composing and playing music, Seymour Perrott, Sir Walford Davies, Gracie of course and Craxton and Farjeon. Various records were played, by way of illustrating, *I Hate You, Croon to Me, Love is Ev'rywhere* and other items from films. What is notable about Harry's speaking voice is how close it is to Perowne's, namely mainly standard clearly articulated BBC Kensington. Occasionally there is very slight variation showing his Welsh background, but no more that his sister 'Billie' in later interviews.

Gracie for her part went off to Capri for rest before her wedding to Monty, held in California on 19 March.

Come Out to Play This typical lavish revue was written and devised by Eddie Pola and Peter Watson. Harry was among a group of lyricists and composers - Eddie Pola, Sonnie Hale, (also director) Harry and Ben Frankel. Harry contributed 3 items, the title song, *Come Out to Play, Thing are going to be Different and Lucky Me, Lucky You.*

> This last song (again e flat and 4/4 time) is a perky number, well suited to the light cabaret style of Matthews, for which Harry supplied words and music, it has a 5-bar introduction, picking up a down stepping phrase from near the end of refrain, ending with short flourish. He verse has 2 long phrases starting off-beat, but running along around the tonic. The 32-bar refrain continues with a more jaunty beginning, which settles into loner phrases to return in last bars and ending with return to key. Altogether more 30's with no undercurrent of yearning, but without the vigour Gracie Harry gave Gracie's songs.

---

[72] Dundee Evening Telegraph, Derby Daily Telegraph 5 February

The show was primarily a vehicle (with supporting cast) for comic compère Sonnie Hale, (who directed it) and for singer/dancer Jessie Matthews (his second wife). It opened at *Phoenix Theatre,* London on 19 March 1940 (the day Monty and Gracie got married), closing in December.

Band Waggon. On March 23, this Gainsborough fllm, *Band Waggon* was released. It was a vehicle, directed by Marcel Vernel. for Arthur Askey and fellow comedian Richard ('Dickie) Murdoch, the mainstays of BBC radio series of broadcasts of the same name. . Basically a loosely framed road film, if mildly subversive, it allows for lots of comic incidents, solo spots for stars like Patricia Kirkwood, an is finally spiced up with some anti-Nazi thriller business.

Because the comic pair are ignored by the BBC, they move off to Sussex, gathering other performers on the way. They all stop at a supposedly haunted castle which in fact houses television equipment capable of sending messages to the enemy. They hi-jack this for a broadcast of a variety show by Arthur and company which triumphantly blocks BBC transmissions to the nation.

Harry was the most notable of the group of composers who provided music, arranged by noted BBC broadcaster, Louis Levy. His one song to sentimental lyrics is from his current staple lyricists Barbara Gordon and Basil Thomas. It is a ballad in imitation Hollywood style. The recording made at the time, features Pat Kirkwood (for whom it was written) and a chorus singing in a style which came to be known as that of 'the MGM heavenly chorus'. In fact it is a very run-of-the –mill typical wartime love song.

They were back to France the following April. From May onwards through June the Germans occupied this part of France and on their return, Gracie and Harry were quickly off to cross the Atlantic.

CHAPTER 9

CANADA TOUR (1940-1)

—————◈—————

The Dominion of Canada supported the UK and of course came to be actively involved in World War II. The Canadian Naval League of Canada formed in 1898 now under its President D.H. Gibson actively sought to operate 24 hostels in various port areas, such as the Sea Gull Cub in Halifax, provide amenities for the Royal Canadian Navy and Canadian Merchant Navy and supply special clothing for visiting seamen.[73]

Gracie had already arrived in Canada on 13 June.[74] To meet up with her Harry boarded the Canadian Pacific liner, the 'Duchess of Bedford'in Liverpool on 24 June 1940, bound for Montreal - the beginning of a tour to raise funds for the *League*.

In Toronto a welcome was given by Mayor and populace on the afternoon of their arrival. The press focussed however on Johnny Weismuller

---

[73]   Cf. www.navyleague.ca

[74]   The Argus (Melbourne) 15 June 1940

visiting a hospital. Their indifferent attitude was further revealed. when Gracie (and (Harry) were only given a 15 minute spot in the concert. Harry smouldered with rage. *If it were me,* he said icily, *I'd give 'em oompah oompah, stick it up your jumpah, and walk straight off.* …….. Gracie more wisely remarked afterwards *I sang with all the confidence and courage I'd been given that afternoon. I sang with everything I had in me to give. At the end of fifteen minutes I just stood there and let the applause roll. Then I went to my dressing-room.* Harry then timed the actual applause, it lasted 10 minutes. He became very angry again. *You think of nothing but your blasted audience.* Eventually he was soothed down. She told them she was going to appear at the *Massey Hall* for the *Navy League* and proceeded to give 5 concerts there. Later during a radio interview, Gracie told the interviewer that Harry had been her accompanist for 10 years. He in a finicky frame of mind, felt compelled to correct her and the interviewer by saying it was nine and a half years. *So you want to split hairs. Yes,* Harry shouted, *for all the radio network to hear.*[75]

They gave a further 6 concerts arranged across the nation, which entailed a lot of travel, which tired them both. Harry continued to grumble about the poor quality of the pianos, At Port Arthur Harry could not be roused while he slept in the railway carriage. A brass band procession awoke the town with its welcome to Gracie - and eventually him!

They travelled to California to stay with Gracie's parents in the house she had bought for them in Santa Monica They needed a break. By late July they were back again in Canada on 7 August to give 3 more concerts in British Columbia and a gala in Vancouver. By 16 August, they were in Regina, Saskachewn for the local branch of the Navy League.[76]

Back home *Black Velvet* started a provincial tour on 21 August at Nottingham Empire Theatre and another revue opened in 4 September.

---

[75]   Gracie Fields, *Sing as We Go, The Autobiography of Gracie Fields, 1960,* Frederick Muller p. 148

[76]   From concert programme

Gracie and Harry with Mounties in Canada

Top of the World For this Charles B Cochrane revue by George Black at the London Palladium, Harry joined with experienced composer Kenneth Leslie-Smith. His contribution was: *Alone with You, Fount of Wisdom, Love Stay in My Heart, My Kind of Music, My Wish,* We'll Go Smiling Along,* (words Phil Park*) What Would You Do, Where the Blue Begins*, Why Worry*, Yet Another Day**. Essentially a vehicle for the Crazy Gang with Pat Kirkwood and Tommy Trinder, it was a sure recipe for success.

The story line was somewhat topical about a barrage-balloon squadron where a balloon broke loose and drifted to another planet ruled over by an extra-terrestrial queen played by Pat Kirkwood. Although it opened on 4 September, due to heavy bombing closed 4 days later; the songs marked * above were salvaged and used in 1944 musical *Jenny Jones*.

> *Love Stay in My Heart* is one of Harry's most haunting melodies. Ater a slow introduction and verse, it moves into a Viennese waltz for its refrain. It looks forward to other waltzes in later musicals. *Love Stay in My Heart*

Sailors Three This was an Ealing Studio's film vehicle for comedian Tommy Trinder released on 14 December. He portrays Tommie Taylor) in farcical situations similar to those in George Formby films. It was directed by Walter Ford and produced by Michael Balcon. Its screenplay was by Austin Melford a frequent writer of comic material, John Dighton and Angus McPhail. Made to seem semi-documentary, it featured a number of established and up-and-coming character actors: Jeanne De Casalis (Mrs Pilkington), Claude Hulbert (Llewellyn Davies 'The Admiral'), John Laurie (McNab), and Michael Wilding (Johnny Wilding). Music was composed and conducted by Ernest Irving with Harry and Noel Gay each contributing a song.

> Harry's was to Phil Park's lyrics, *Singing a Happy Go Lucky Song,* yet another jollification song, made for Trinder's bluff and cheery personality and voice.

> Harry wrote another Capri song published sometime during 1940, *My Capri Sserenade* with a mild Latin flavour. It would be easy to read this to be from the words he wrote a lament for Gracie's presence. With a slow Latin American beat, it has no verse, but has a short theme in the introduction repeated throughout the song as a kind of musical mantra - *Play my Capri Serenade.* The whole vocal line is repeated, leading to a coda with a new phrase repeated to make a sustained climax.

> More unexpected was a tribute to Her Majesty Queen Elizabeth with words by Phil Park *Here's to the Queen (God Bless Her).* This could well have stimulated by her *sang froid* in the teeth of her home Buckingham Palace being bombed on 13 September. It is very much in the British style of vocalised slow march, particularly reminiscent of Eric Coates and William Walton. After the slow introduction, the melody rises with sonorous chords. The verse is a slow almost ponderous melody,. The refrain has a much more regular pattern, followed by drum roll pattern in the melody, before it returns to the first tune again, which is repeated with a brief roll-call.

Harry only seems to have written the one published song this year, the well written nostalgic *It Always Rains Before the Rainbow* to words by actor Gordon Orbell and himself. The verse with some effective echoing effects has sentiments about the sunrise. The refrain in a fox-trot tempo takes up the title as prefiguring future hope for the future when the absent lover returns. For the next five years he wrote no more individual published songs, he was so busy.

Chapter 10

'TROOPER' DAVIES (1941- 1942)

Early in the next year 1941 Harry was involved with another new Black review:-

Gangway It was produced by Robert Nesbitt with a variety of sketches, solo acts and set dances of 8 items, an intermission and a further 9 items. It featured Bebe Daniels and Ben Lyon, performers from BBC Radio series, popular comedian Tommy Trinder, the singing duo Anne Ziegler and Webster Booth.. Harry contributed 3 numbers with lyrics by Barbara Gordon and Basil Thomas plus an arrangement. Veteran composer Noel Gay wrote 2 songs and former lyricist Phil Park one. Two of Harry's songs opened the show – the title song *Gangway,* for the company followed by a song for Bebe Daniels and Ben Lyon *You Annoy Me.*

A change in Mood for the 4th item – a sketch *Shangri-La.* where Webster Booth is cast as the Wanderer and Anne Zeigler as His Heart's Desire, surrounded by Maidens of the Pool. For this Harry provides the duo with *My Paradise.* A sumptuously romantic song, it starts off with a short loud introduction and the voice quickly enters its long line of melody, outlining his quest. The refrain is a tango, which would not of been out-of -place for the Red Shadow in *The Desert Song*, its melody making the mood one of determination, changing tempo and key until a climactic note. This resolves into a repeat of the refrain.

The sheet music puts it firmly in the tenor-high baritone range as a solo. The recording however sounds as if taken directly from the show has a long cadenza for Anne to sing rather shrilly before the verse sets under way with Webster's tenor entry. The tango refrain becomes an acceptably harmonised duet with Webster singing the harmony.

Harry also provided a vocal duet arrangement for them of a Chopin Ētude, Opus 10. No.3 Tristesse *How Deep is the Night* as part of a medley of music in the Act 1 finale.[77] Again the music was arranged by Debroy Somers who conducted his Orchestra.

The delay from doing compulsory national military service now came to an end. An application for enlistment 1 August was sent to the War Office from Lieutenant-Colonel Francis Gordon Lane Fox, Scots Guards, Household Cavalry Motor Training Battalion at the Hyde Park Barracks. He wrote:-

Harry Parr-Davies

Authority is required please for the enlistment of the above-named man into the Band of the Life Guards. He has been medically examined and graded A.2., which precludes him from enlisting into the Household Cavalry under the existing regulations.

As this man is an accomplished musician (he is in fact Composer and Accompanist to Miss Gracie Fields), I feel that his service would be an asset to my band and, although there is no vacancy in the Band at the moment, I am prepared to transfer an A.I man from the Band to duty.

I should be grateful if this matter could be treated as urgent

---

[77]   Cf.20 December HMV record D 9247, *So Deep in the Night*.

(SD.) F LANE FOX[78].

The process to enlist him had been started by Captain Albert Lemoine, the Band's Director of Music from 1938. He wished to incorporate able musicians into the Band. Two other musicians came from the London Symphony Orchestra, - Jock Ashby, its principal trombone and Dennis MacManson, violinist.

On 13 August 1941, Harry now 27 years of age was enlisted (as no. 295736) and posted to *His Majesty's Lifeguards* under Lemoine. *Captain Lemoine, now with the opportunity of enlisting top civilian musicians, transferred four junior members to line regiments to create vacancies. One of the new intake was Harry Parr Davies.... Musician Parr Davies was highly thought of by Captain Lemoine and was given the doubtful privilege of being permitted to smoke during rehearsals.*

Harry gave his address at the time, not as a London hotel or Swansea with his family but Penmaen Hall, a small residential Hotel on the Gower Peninsula, where he had gone for peace and quiet to work on his music.

As it turned out his army residential base was handily in Knightsbridge. In the event, it meant that he was near when Gracie performed London concert halls, like the Albert Hall, or with ENSA or for the morale-boosting. In addition he remained close to the West End for whatever revue (or later musical) He was in the process of seeing musicals safely launched on the stage. Nationally and locally, they were important morale boosters not only for the beleaguered Britain. Even before he started an initial drill training of 5-6 weeks, he was playing at a concert on 17 August with different bands and popular soloists. Gracie sang as top of the bill, accompanied by Harry now listed as a Trooper.

---

[78]   Household Cavalry Museum and Archive Records of Harry's enlistment August 1941

Albert Hall concert programme

"Trooper" Harry at piano with Gracie

As he was not part of the mounted section of the band, he had no need of further cavalry training. Indeed Harry was rather devious. He booked in at the Dorchester Hotel, bribing a Corporal to clean his boots and buttons. This stopped when his Colonel-in-Chief found out.[79]

A decision was made to move the Life Guards. *In late 1941 the Band moved west to Combermere Barracks, Windsor, but still carried out engagements in the London parks and seaside resorts, now wearing the drab khaki battledress.*[80] The band produced gramophone records during the war. Furthermore, they broadcast frequently throughout the war on the BBC Home and Forces Programme and later on the Light Programme.

After joining up, the earliest broadcast he could have been involved as a member of the Band was at 2-2.30 pm 2 October on the BBC Forces programme. Such a half-an-hour spot was typical. Harry was ill during November, which meant a re-scheduling of 7 November BBC Forces Programme until later 21 November.[81] Then he made a BBC Home Service at 9.20 'The Story of Gracie Fields' with Bert Aza.[82]

Harry on occasion featured as a soloist with the military band or more likely played as part of the dance band formed from its members, when not involved with ENSA and Gracie.

> True to form, he penned a couple of songs - one by his former lyricists, Roma Campbell-Hunter, *Lonely Serenade*. It was featured by Lew Stone who led a 7-piece band at the Dorchester Hotel. It is a typical waltz tune of the time, it starts in C for the verse, which has a repeated rocking motif. Unusually for Harry, he changes to another key (F) for its refrain ending on its repeat with a partly hummed partly sung final 8 bars.

---

[79] Gracie Fields, *Sing as We Go, The Autobiography of Gracie Fields, 1960,* Frederick Muller *p. 108*

[80] George R Lawn, 1995, *Music in State Clothing the story of the Kettledrummers, Trumpeters and Band of the Lifeguards,* Lee Cooper, p.45 and 6

[81] 7 November, Nottingham Evening Post

[82] 21 November Yorkshire Evening Post

Similarly, he finds another way of using the contemporary idiom, where he asks for the refrain to be 'In a ballad style' in *It Always Rains Before the Rainbow.* Gordon Orbell and Harry provide the conventionally uplifting lyrics. He opens the phrases echoed an octave higher. He repeats this echo effect when the voice enters. This leads by contrast into a more strict tempo refrain which is similar to earlier upbeat numbers for Gracie.

Once 1942 was ushered in, Harry was busy with a round of films, revues and as well as band duties and was at the height of his powers.

Dates in footnotes below are taken from newspaper notices of the Band's Broadcasts on BBC while Harry was enlisted with them. Programmes usually lasted 30-45 minutes. As they do not include programme details, it is not known whether Harry played during any particular broadcast. However they do not clash with other known dates where he was performing other than band duties. For instance there was a half-hour Band concert on Forces Programme on 12 February.

Happidrome

Harry contributed lyrics to the stage version of the radio comedy show *Happidrome* staged at the *Prince of Wales Theatre.* This was produced by Jack Buchanan. It starred Mr. Lovejoy (Harry Korris) the theatre proprietor Ramsbottom (Cecil Frederick) his stage manager, Enoch (Robbie Vincent) the gormless call-boy, plus Leslie Hutchinson (as himself) and "Two Ton" Tessie O'Shea, another virtuoso ukelele player a kind of female George Formby. This had as musical director Paul Fenouhlet who also wrote some of the songs. It had a longer than usual out of West End try-out, appearing on 23 November at *New Cross Empire.* He wrote 2 songs for Hutch to sing as a guest performer in a variety programme in the farcical stage helter-skelter background to the show a pleasant enough slow fox-trot in Harry's more automatic style, tailored for Hutch's voice and range *You are My Love Song.* This is followed as a mild contrast by a brighter quick-step, *Take the World Exactly As You Find It.* It was filmed by MGM and released on 7 June 1943.

Full Swing During this year, he was given a London posting, which meant he was nearer the heart of the West End scene. Therefore at the end of 1941, despite axis hostilities being at their height, Harry was invited to develop further his musical range. For this his first musical since the *Curfew* in his youth, he joined experienced fellow composers George Posford and Kenneth Leslie-Smith, but it was Harry who contributed the lion's share of songs. Posford did 2 and Leslie-Smith 1 to Harry's 7 numbers, but not as yet the full score as he did in many subsequent musicals. The lyricists were Barbara Gordon and Basil Thomas.

The show staged at the *Palace Theatre* on 16 April was created for the lively West-End husband and wife comedy partnership, Jack Hulbert (Jack Millett) and Cicely Courtneidge (Kay Porter) They played a married film star team, playing the same characters from a earlier success, *Under Your Hat* which had music by Vivian Ellis. The script in this musical as in the earlier show gives them scope to enter into a number of disguises when they are set to work on an implausible secret mission for the War Office. This involves tracking down state secrets and missing dossiers of villainous Dr. Carlos in Rio de Janeiro, where most of the musical is set. Harry provided the title song *Full Swing* for the Hulberts on stage at the Palace Theatre, London – they used the device of a theatre in a theatre – and again in the finale scene in the Estoril Theatre in Rio.

Harry wrote 2 comic numbers for Jack Hulbert, *Shopping, Eating and The Nine O'Clock News* and *You Only Want It 'Cos You Haven't Got It*. The latter is a witty and lively song, basically the well-tried formula of an introduction, comic verses and a tag-like refrain incorporating the title. With lyrics from Max Kester and Barbara Gordon, Harry gives Cecily, *Music Makes Me Mad*. For Gabrielle Brune (Sally) he has 3 songs to lyrics by Barbara Gordon and Basil Thomas *Follow My Dancing Feet*. A charming tale of uplift is provided by a songbird, which causes the singer to start dancing in the refrain to a folk-like tune, saying how beneficent nature is to tunes reminiscent of earlier folk songs like *Over the Hills and Far Away*. Then there was *Love is Love Everywhere* and *Mamma, Buy Me That* - a kind of torch song with an apparently innocent child-like pseudo-classical beginning, with some ominous phrases in the bass-line. This moves into the refrain which is song absolutely about getting what you want, the insistent ironic style akin to Kurt Weill's *The Saga of Jenny* in the musical, 1941 *Lady in the Dark*, but made somehow typical of Harry at his wittiest.

Under the management of Tom Arnold and Lee Ephraim with costumes by Doris Zinkeisen, it opened for the usual provincial test run at the *Opera House,* Blackpool 18 February 1942. It moved then for 2 weeks of performances to Liverpool, 2 in Manchester, 2 in Glasgow before returning to Blackpool on 11 April. It quickly transferred to *London's Palace Theatre* for a successful run of 468 performances, closing on 29 May 1943. After this, the show again went on provincial tour during early 1944 with Jack Warner and Marie Marion in the Hulbert leads.[83]. After this show, Harry provided complete scores on his own, except for the next Cicely Courtneidge vehicle in 1949. In addition to this first musical, Harry now collaborated on two more revues, wrote a song for a film and another for inclusion in a musical revival in addition to his band duties.

Big Top. The first revue was another Charles B Cochran very extensive production in 25 scenes in 2 parts. It opened on 8 May at *His Majesty's Theatre.* It had all-rounder singer-actress Patricia Burke with established favourites - in particular Fred Emney, Australian character actor and singer, Cyril Ritchard with his wife and long time partner Madge Elliott, Gretchen Franklin and especially transatlantic comedic performer Beatrice Lillie and a young Pearl Carr in bit parts, (who later teamed up with Teddy Johnson as the popular vocal duo).

Harry as usual was one of several contributors of music including Nicholas Brodzsky and Geoffrey Wright (with whom Harry wrote the opening song *Getting Rid of It* to lyrics by Herbert Farjeon). His more usual lyricists at this time Barbara Gordon and Basil Thomas and they wrote the other words in the show for Harry's songs. In Scene 3, *Tin Pan Alley,* there was *Pluggers Lament* for Patricia Burke. He had nothing more until Part II, Scene 19, quickly paced *Hey Ho* for Patricia Burke and singers Cyril Ritchard, Madge Elliot.

The next scene 20, *the Lady in Grey,* featured one of the best of Harry's more serious songs for Beatrice Lillie *Wind Round My Heart.* The verse meditates on the winter weatherwhich chimed in with singer's mood of isolation. The refrain is more dynamic about the wind portrayed as emotional pain with restless changes of tempo and key and the restless

---

[83] Kurt Ganzl, 1986, *The British Musical Theatre* 1915-1984, Macmillan Press, p. 516-7/520-1

harmonic shifts which are particularly effective. Not to lose the intensity, the refrain is not repeated. The song subsides on a long held note.

For scene 24, he gives Patricia Burke a song with a male chorus *When I hear Music*. There was much additional music from USA and elsewhere arranged by Ben Frankel, the distinguished composer who conducted the Orchestra.

Suspected Person This was an Associated British Picture Corporation thriller. film released in June 1942. Following a $50,000 bank New York Robbery, suspects Franklin (Robert Beatty) and Dolan (Eric Clavering) are acquitted by a USA court. They journey to England in the belief that the money is in possession of crook-turned-reporter Jim Raynor (Clifford Evans). He has tried to exchange it from dollars to sterling. Inspector Thompson of Scotland Yard (David Farrar) knowing the suspects are in Britain, goes undercover by moving into Raynor's apartment let by Raynor's sister, Joan (Patricia Roc). Harry provided a song *Every Night at Seven*. This is a typically film noir night-club slow swing number, like David Raskin's *Laura* with words by Barbara Thomas.

> It is a simple piece in structure, simply introduction, no verse or refrain just a long melody in which the words *Every Night at Seven* of the title are repeated as a kind of mantra. Such a well-crafted song shows how Harry was developing his compositional techniques. The song deserves to be better known.

He was given leave for a week from 14 to 21 September, whether holiday due or illness, the purpose is not given in his record.[84] The band recorded Columbia DB 2081 *Tommies Tunes* in 2 parts and gave a further concert for BBC Forces Programme at 10-30 -11pm on 12 December.

Cheltenham

Besides all this compositional and accompanying activity, Harry appeared as a soloist. Probably as a more local attempt to keep Gloucestershire 'chins up', there was a festival in from 2 to 8 August held in the gracious Montpellier Square Cheltenham. *The Band of His Majesty's Lifeguards*

---

[84] Household Cavalry Museum and Archive Records of Harry's service

gave concerts conducted by Lieutenant-Colonel Albert Lemoine (their Bandmaster from 1938 to 1959) on Sunday 2 August and each afternoon, Harry played the solo piano part in Richard Addinsell's popular wartime piece *The Warsaw Concerto*.[85]

While there he was elected to the committee of the *Performing Rights Society* to replace Arthur Tate, who had retired due to ill-health and is remembered chiefly for the charming ballad *Somewhere a voice is calling*.[86] The Performing Rights Society had been formed in 1914, by publishers Boosey and Hawkes to protect the rights of musicians lyricist and publishers. Harry could well have joined the Society in early 1930's. There was Band recording, this time for Columbia, done on 21 October with a two-part title, *Tommies Tunes.*

Best Bib & Tucker This revue opened on 7 November at the London Palladium in the usual 2 acts, with 6 scenes before intermission and 7 after. It was developed by Black as a vehicle for self-centred comedian Tommy Trinder. It was notable for Trinder's 'take off' of Carmen Miranda (Carmen Minranda!) - a song *No, No, No, Columbus,* written by Val Guest with Edmundo Ross and his orchestra in a Cuban set. Harry provided the music for the 2 opening numbers, *Gentlemen of Leisure* and the title song. Another piece was by Herman Finck and based on the Rev. Richard Harris Barham classic Victorian poem, *the Jackdaw of Rheims.* It ran for 490 performances. Harry contributed the opening songs, one was the title song, the other called *Gentlemen of Leisure.*

Belle of New York This was a revival of the early American musical by Emile Littler which opened on 23 December 1942 at the London Coliseum, featuring Edith Stamp-Taylor.

Harry was one of two who provided music, his was an insert waltz song, *Love Alone Will Remain* for the heroine. It is a quiet exposition of contented love for musical personality comedy lead in the show Evelyn Laye.

---

[85]   Cheltenham Chronicle

[86]   News in brief, 7 August 1942

After all this activity, Harry pleaded with Gracie for some respite from accompanying her saying that he was exhausted. This was not to be. Unfortunately 1943 saw even more activity for Harry on all fronts, films, musical and band programmes.

CHAPTER 11

NEW MUSICALS (1943)

Women aren't Angels This is a film based in one of the many Aldwych stage farces. Stalwarts Robertson Hare and Alfred Drayton regularly appeared in them. This film was released on the 18 January by Associated British Picture Corporation (ABCP) with Lawrence Huntington as director shows them in a suitably zany plot. Timorous Wilmer Popday (Robertson Hare) and more dominant Arthur Bandle (Alfred Drayton) are partners in a music publishing firm and friends outside of work. The pair also in the Home Guard get into trouble from their respective wives Thelma and Elizabeth who have joined the Auxiliary Territorial Service (ATS) when Bandle is late for a party before the women return from leave. He had given a girlfriend a lift. Popday promises the wives he'll restrain his errant friend, but Bandle has a mind of his own. Left to their own devices and at a loose end, the men become involved in a spy ring and a beautiful spy and decide to dress up in their wives' ATS uniforms. Hare gets to use his usual catch phrase "Oh calamity". In a typical incident, they try to get a lift by showing off their legs. When Hare takes off his (her) cap in gratitude, he shows his bald head. The driver speeds off. The plot moves on to various marital and other predicaments. While Charles Williams did the music arrangements, Harry wrote a song *My Kind of Loving*. For this Harold Purcell provided the words. This marked the beginning of partnership which lasted until Harry's death. Harold Purcell was 7 years older than Harry and had a lot of experience writing for films as well as plays for the stage.

We'll Meet Again Released by Columbia British Productions on 18 January 1943 in UK, this was an unsophisticated showtime vehicle featuring Vera Lynn and her singing. It was directed by Philip Brandon with screenplay by James Seymour and Howard Thomas (script contribution), The plot is a simple tale of success in World War II London for a young female dancer named Peggy Brown, (Vera Lynn) who very surprisingly finds she can sing! Reluctant to perform, she nevertheless entertains a packed theatre during an air raid singing one of her early classics, *Be Like The Kettle And Sing*.

Peggy's friend composes classical music, but he doesn't like "that popular music rubbish". However, for Peggy he starts composing popular music! The song he writes turns out to be satisfactory and she ends up singing it on a recording with Geraldo's Band. By mistake it is played by the BBC. The result is she begins to introduce a weekly radio series (as in real life she did with her radio series 'Sincerely Yours'). She becomes a kind of 'agony aunt', taking a young depressed lad she knows to a friend of hers in the country. He decides he likes it there and stays on. She also manages to get a formerly engaged couple back together after they have differed. The girl has his baby while he is serving away. Sending her good wishes to the couple on the air, she hears he has been killed in action – a cue for Harry's *All the World Sings a Lullaby*.

> Harry uses the usual song structure in a different way. He writes a slow waltz, with an introduction, a short verse with a long refrain. He keeps the vocal range comparatively narrow. Vera Lynn's voice is very clear in tone and diction and always accurate in pitch, but can sound rather hard in its upper reaches. Harry avoids this by keeping it in the warmer lower part of her voice. After a rocking almost Mozartian introduction, not related to what comes after in the vocal line, he gives Vera a gentle soothing melody. It is a charming number akin to *Tree Top Lullaby* 10 years before.

The lad in fact has just been injured, so all ends happily The film naturally ends with Vera singing *We'll Meet Again*.

Police Ball

On 6 March a Ball was held in Gloucester Guildhall for Gloucester City Police. This was in aid of the Red Cross Prisoner of War Fund and Longford Children's Hospital. The band played, with Harry as soloist for the 300 guests. It raised £60.[87] The band had a busy year with 15 BB radio broadcasts. It is not clear how many times Harry appeared during his time with the Band or its dance band section, nor of course how much rehearsal time he attended involved as he was not only with the band, sings for film (c.f *Happidrome*) and his West End revues and musicals. [88]

Being engaged to write a complete musical was for Harry a much more elaborate venture than composing songs for films or even scenes for revues, indeed it was more akin to his early work with the *Curfew*.

During a very busy year in 1943, he produced 2 new musicals but as their sole composer. To make the musical work, he had to deal with a wide range of people. Even more than revues, musical comedies (or musicals for short) were intended as a means for telling a story, using the talent available.

---

[87]   Gloucester Citizen 6 March

[88]

23 January	9-9.30 am	Forces Programme
24 March	1.45-2.15pm	Forces Programme
29 March	7.15-7.30 am	Forces Programme
18 April	11-11.30	Forces Programme
10 June	2.15-3 pm	Home Service
10 July	9-9.30 am	Home Service
3 September	10.20-10.45 am	Home Service
11 September	11.00 am	Forces Programme
17 September	9.50-10.15 am	Home Service
19 September	11-11.30am	Forces Programme
17 October	9.50-10.15 am	Home Service
14 November	11-11.30 am	Forces Programme
7 December	12-12.30 pm	Forces Programme
24 December	12-12.30 pm	Forces Programme
26 December	2-2.30 pm	Home Service

The shape of musicals [89]

Musicals derived from the earlier lighter forms of opera as structures. These in turn came from many European sources usually with their own national 'flavour', but could be transferred and popular elsewhere. They included 18th and 19th century Ballad Operas (English and not readily transferable), More widespread were Singspiels (German), Opèras - comique and - bouffes (French) and opera buffa (Italian with harpsichord or piano accompanied recitative based on speech patterns, but stylised). During the 19th century, the operetta (French and Austrian) developed as a more sentimental variant. Musical comedy evolved particularly in USA as a way of incorporating the vigour of revues into a more sustained narrative with the music in the hands of European emigrés or their descendants.

Usual Origins –   i) a play or a novel;

ii) contemporary or historical theme

iii) a biography

iv) a vehicle for a popular entertainer

Available experts Director to oversee; Producer to co-ordinate stage presentation; Costume, scenery and lighting designer; Musical director to coordinate the music required and often orchestrate it; Composer and lyricist able to accommodate and exploit available musical resources, especially choreographer, dancers, singers, chorus conductor and orchestra

Overture Usually this consists of a pot-pourri of salient melodies (as in many opera overtures) linked to form a striking set of contrasts intended to get the audience in the mood for what follows.

Dialogue This is sometimes a pruned version of an earlier original play. Its function is to reveal further aspects of character or explain situations

---

[89]   Kurt Ganzl, 1995, *Musicals,* Carlton, pp 166-168, This book provides a wide view of both the origins of musicals and many significant developments.. Although Harry is not mentioned in it, there is much useful background about the genre of music theatre..

within the plot, to introduce and link musical numbers as well as push the action on. Usually, the emotion in situations is developed in the music. One artifice, melos (or melodrama), used sometimes in mid-19th century French opéra-comique and sparingly in Italian opera, is a device where speech instead of singing has an underlying theme of significance in the orchestra. It can heighten a scene's dramatic effect, e.g. the letter scenes in Verdi's *Macbeth* and *La Traviata* or Cathèrine's recollection of her dead mother in Meyerbeer's *L'Étoile du Nord..* It became very commonplace in films.

Songs, duets, trios and ensembles – The range of the melodies are tailored to be well within the compass of the singers. Their function is to heighten the emotion, humour or characterisation of situation.

Dance is often a feature to provide local colour either of place or time, usually devised by a well known choreographer

Jack Hulbert the experienced director, singer and dancer summed up the whole background needed for a musical: *Opening a big musical is always a daunting task. A straight play is difficult enough in all conscience but with a dancing chorus, a singing chorus, trick lighting, setting up new complicate sets for the first time, making necessary adjustments, band calls and principals, it is no picnic.* [90]

The Knight was Bold This was Harry's first musical comedy fully composed solely by him. In 2 acts, it was originally written by Harriett Jay (as the 1907 farce *When Knights were Bold*. The idea was close to Mark Twain's novel *A Yankee at the Court of King Arthur*). It was now reprocessed by Emile Littler and co-author Thomas Browne, with lyrics and dialogue added by Harry's frequent lyricists at this time Barbara Gordon and Basil Thomas. It was an effort criticised at the time as being too full of mock mediaevalism such as *Thee* and *Thou*.

The first pre-West End performance was at *Theatre Royal*, Newcastle-upon-Tyne on 26 April. 1943, at this stage with odd title of *Kiss the Girls* - making it sound more like vaudeville than musical comedy. Its scenario

---

[90]   Jack Hulbert, 1975, *The Little Woman's Always Right,* W H Allen, p 220

intended as a vehicle for popular West End comedy and musical revue star Sonnie Hale.

It is the tale set in the family seat of the De Vere's at Beechwood Castle. Dean Peter Pottlebury DD and his daughters open the show on the day before the Regatta Day with *Tradition*. His daughters congratulate their father with *Well Done, Dean*. A hard up feckless aristocrat Sir Guy De Vere (Sonnie Hale) appears. He has returned from service in India to inherit the family title and dressed in a dinner suit sings, *I Go on My Way Whistling*. The family relatives and retainers spurn him.

However his cousin the rather stately Lady Rowena Brown (Adele Dixon) is in love with him *If This is Love*. He is in love with her, but very unsure how to declare it. Guy and the Dean's daughters now embark on *Kiss the Girls* (the obvious source of the pre-London title of the show). Sue Lloyd (Enid Stamp-Taylor) an American visitor joins him in *You and the Moonlight*. The act ends with Crecy Charlie and the company in the act 1 finale.

In Act 2 Sir Guy has hit his head and dreams he is back with Rowena in the Middle Ages, now fully clothed in armour The act opens in the castle Battlement with Crecy Charlie and the company singing mock mediaeval *In summer When the Trees Be Green*. Guy follows this up with what was thought to be the show's best number, *Whoopsy Diddle Dum Dee*. He sees himself battling against Sir Brian Ballymote (Fred Kitchen jnr). Guy and Rowena join together in the next 2 numbers, *Where the Rainbow Ends* and *I'm Telling Thee*. Sue and the Dean's daughters do a song and dance number, *Mother Nature* before all complications are solved in the finale.

. The costumes were by talented Doris Zinkeisen and Norman Hartnell among others. The music was conducted by Phil Green and his Orchestra; he did the necessary musical arrangements. Further performances were given at the *Hippodrome* Coventry, *Grand Theatre* Blackpool, *Grand Theatre* Leeds, *Theatre Royal* Birmingham, Liverpool and Edinburgh until 19 June. It then opened on 10 July at the *Piccadilly Theatre*. After a favourable opened night, it only lasted 10 further nights. One song *Halfway to Heaven* was dropped during the provincial tour. [91]

The first London performance on the 1 July 1943 was at the *Piccadilly Theatre,* and the show now retitled as *The Knight was Bold* but with little success only lasting 10 performances. Fortunately, the next musical would be one of his key-works and was very successful. Harold Purcell now provided his lyrics almost exclusively rather than, Phil Park, Barbara Gordon and Basil Thomas.

Lisbon Story George Black gave Harry's next musical an ambitious production with a contemporary war-theme scenario and lyrics by Harold Purcell He used his film experience to give Harry musically a variety of situations to display compositionally different and imaginative styles. Apart from songs and dances, the score included much *melos* both to underpin the dialogue and to anticipate later numbers or reprise earlier numbers. Its use derived from Purcell's experience with filming. Backdrop stills were shown intending to make the atmosphere more realistic and immediate as in *cinema-verité.*

Debroy Somers did the necessary musical arrangement - hence the conventional pot-pourri overture, arranged from 8 of the show's songs with the waltz song as a climax. [92] The opening scene of Act 1 shows Gabrielle's studio in July 1938 Paris where friends and associates have cameo roles to create a suitable artistic atmosphere around Gabrielle Girard, (Patricia Burke) a famous Parisian singer.

After a brief orchestral introduction (No. 1) based on first song her friend Stephan Gorelle picks up the tune on the piano. Humming this Panache another friend (Noelle Gordon)[93] sings the first song (No. 2) a bright soubrette number *Happy Days*. At first Gorelle accompanies her on the piano at the beginning of the verse, the refrain follows to a strict tempo quickstep, setting out the sentiments of its title. Gabrielle

---

[91]   It is difficult to evaluate the musical as there is no score or sheet music available. High farce is not really Harry's scene- he is best at the more romantic/ nostalgic numbers.

[92]   This is different to Harry's MS in Parr–Davies collection.

[93]   She later became famous playing the motel owner in TV soap, *Crossroads*

loves Englishman, David Warren (a non-singing part for Jack Livesey) who works in the British Foreign Office. No. 3 is a melos, introducing Gabrielle's first song (No. 4) a waltz a song of farewell to David *Someday We Shall Meet Again*. In the verse, she ponders on the present before the big tune (reminiscent of Ivor Novello). The entr'acte repeats (no.4) this as an orchestral interlude.

The scene changes to her Villa in neutral Lisbon in summer 1942. Gabrielle .has escaped from the German Occupation of France to come here. The musical intention is to use songs, dances and music to give an Iberian atmosphere. The chorus sings a mock-Latin American comedy number *Madame Louisa* which has many off-beat entries from Lola (Margaret McGrath) a local singer. She delights in retailing Madame Louisa's many faults and international escapades in verse 1 and 2. The crowd disperses as the music for the song turns into a dance.

The scene changes to a Lisbon street. Gonzalez a fruit seller (high tenor Joseph Dollinger) sings a nostalgic waltz-song *Never Say Goodbye* (no. 7) which Gabrielle hears and embellishes with graceful runs. At the end of it, Gabrielle (no. 7a) reprises it expressing her longing for David.

A brief melos features the tune under dialogue between Gestapo Carl von Schiner (Albert Lieven in another no-singing part; he often played Nazi Officers in British wartime films) and his assistant Doctor Hoffman from the Berlin Cultural Department. They admire Gabrielle and plot what she can do for then.

More dialogue continues over the introduction of the next song a vaguely tango rhythm which Ramon, (Ronaldo Mazar) a street singer embarks on the charming *Music at Midnight*. The scene ends with yet another melos (No. 8) using orchestrally *Someday We'll Meet Again* under the dialogue.

Gabrielle has been approached by von Schriner. If she returns Paris, he will arrange for her to appear in a suitable piece of musical theatre - an operetta, *La Comtesse*. She agrees to this because it can provide a front to assist the escape to Britain of a French scientist and his daughter. The scientist is developing an important new metal. Gabrielle will act the role of the daughter's designer in the operetta.

During a further scene change to the Lisbon quayside, but using a harbour back-drop, the *Vincent Tildsley Mastersingers* dressed as Portuguese fisher folk mending their nets sing *Pedro the Fisherman* (no. 10). (The need for this emerged during the out of town trail run, which started on 3 May at Imperial Theatre in Brighton for 2 weeks. By the 3rd night the time taken to do the change from Paris to Lisbon was noticeable. Purcell and Davies wandered back to their hotel in a blitz warning, with the composer whistling a mite disconsolately. Why not have out a whistling song to cover the scene change? Apparently written on scraps of paper by the fourth night in Brighton, the resultant chorus went into the show). The chorus fulfils its function well. It has a core set of verses and tunes lasting about 4 mins long. (In the vocal score more verses can be added should more time be needed). Somewhat ironically the show is best remembered for this whistling tune which sold 50,000 song copies in a week. The record of the basic set of verses made by the *Vincent Tildsley Mastersingers* was BBC Radio's most frequent request at the time.

The curtain is raised while an organ is heard off-stage playing a hymn-like andante. The fisher folk go into church singing a harmonised but wordless chorus (No. 11a) and process to bless the fleet. Once this is over, Carmelita (Nora Savage) a singer (of coloratura ability) sings a short Spanish-flavoured waltz (No. 11b) *Carnival Song* as a prelude to a sequence of *cor de ballet* pieces with an Iberian flavour, although nearer to Latin America in tone than Portugal (No. 11c). They start with a slow but lilting Spanish waltz which leads to an increasingly noisy climax with two key changes on the way. A Festival dance (No. 11d) follows as a feature for 2 of Gabrielle's friends (the distinguished Polish duo Alicia Halama and Ciesław Konarski). Another dance sequence starts slowly and lyrically again changing to a bolero and a slow waltz, which accelerates coming to a lively conclusion. The villagers leave (No. 12). Von Schriner has found out who the scientist is. He will turn a blind eye if Gabrielle becomes his lover

The act closes with a set number (No. 13) for Gabriel *Song of the Sunrise*. The verse views the present in a hesitant line, while the refrain indicates hope for the future in a typical flowing tune by Harry, the chorus entering in harmony supporting Gabrielle's voice. She leaves with von Shriner for Paris.

Act II begins in a railway station setting on the border between Spain and France. Ramon sings *Serenade for Sale,* (No. 14) a vocalised tango in a tongue-in-cheek style reminiscent of Friml's *Donkey Serenade.* Gorelle, Gabrielle's friend, picks it up in a burlesque way (No. 14a) to which the chorus respond by harmonising briefly (No. 14b). As Gabrielle departs, a melos (No. 15) reprises the waltz *Someday We'll Meet Again* and the scene ends with the chorus reprising (No. 16) *Never Say Goodbye.* A final melos reprises *Someday* ending with music portraying a train in motion, topped with a vibraphone signifying Radio Berlin broadcasting. They are on their way to Paris.

The well-used device of a show within a show heralds the first performance of the operetta at the *Théâtre Mogador.*[94] Gabrielle takes the place of the scientist's daughter as a boy. This allows the scientist and his daughter time to be hurried away to safety in England.

The rehearsal of the operetta on stage starts with music for a scene change (No. 18) called 'Mogador Theatre'. Then the story moves back to Gabrielle's studio Paris when Gabrielle's friends, Panache and Gorelle, reprise *Happy Days* as duet (No. 19).

The actual extended finale of Act I of 'La Comtesse' (No. 20) entitled somewhat grandly 'Napoleonic Scena' follows.[95] The men of the chorus start by marching into a festive Paris to a rhythmic tune in Romberg style *So Paris Wears Her Easter Dress.* The number contains solos for four characters by way of interludes during the march - first a Soldier (high tenor Joseph Dollinger) talks about dreaming; secondly a Milkmaid (high soprano Nora Savage) sings a waltz about Paris being special; thirdly an Innkeeper (baritone Kurt Wagener) sings for people to encourage them all to drink and lastly a Flower Girl (Eleanor Fayre) reprises *Never Say Good Bye* as a duet with the Soldier. A brief fully harmonized reprise of *Some Day We Shall Meet Again* follows this. A reveille is sounded; the Drummer Boy (Patricia Burke) enters to a march, *Follow the Drum,* which the chorus take up. The march continues without chorus (No. 21) as the company marches off. After this there is a snatch of *Happy Days* as the scene changes.

---

[94]   This is an actual theatre founded in 1913 and still producing musicals!

[95]   Surely there is some unconscious irony here choosing the Napoleonic era, 'Boney' being the Hitler of his day!

Backstage, Gorelle is playing the piano as he and Lisette sing a brief duet (No.22) *April in the Spring of Love.*

(No.23) is a line of bridging music after dialogue introduces the ballet (No.24), set as a type of morality play. Evil (Konarski) tempts and seduces Innocence (Eleonor Fayre) despite the presence of Piety (Alicia Halama) and Wisdom (Patricia Burke). Wisdom steps forward at the end to point up the moral of the ballet.

Once Gabrielle's deceit has been discovered, von Schriner shoots Gabrielle dead and the *Marseillaise* (No. 25) is sung in defiance, making a thrilling and moving *coup de théâtre.* It ends with a triumphant harmonised (No.26) *Someday We Shall Meet Again* as a final curtain.

Once put on at the *London Hippodrome* [96] by George Black on 17 June 1943 and drew large audiences running for 492 performances. Rather ironically as a kind of German reply to it, it ended its run abruptly on 8 July 1944 when the devastation resulting from German V-1 'flying bombs' [97] forced the majority of London's theatrical venues to shut temporarily. Nevertheless, after only three months on tour it returned to the Stoll Theatre on 17 October for a further 54 performances with Maria Eisler as Gabrielle and other small cast changes. It closed on 2 December 1944, [98] but then set on a provincial tour. During this tour, Harry added to a new song for Lisette after *Music at Midnight Very Odd Fish.*[99]

Finally at the Grand Armistice Ball held on 11 November in Gloucester by dance band section of His Majesty's Life Guards, Harry was the piano soloist.[100]

---

[96]   Harry later said he preferred this London theatre cf Welsh Rarebit' interview, summer 1949

[97]   Rex Walford 2004, *Harry Parr Davies,* Oxford Dictionary of National Biography, p. 369

[98]   Kurt Ganzl, 1986, *The British Musical Theatre* 1915-1984, Macmillan Press, p. 528-9/539-40

[99]   Programme – Liverpool Empire 24 Sept 1945

[100]   Gloucester Citizen 8 November 1943

CHAPTER 12

THE LATER WAR YEARS (1944-1946)

Harry started off 1944 with music for 3 films.

Bell Bottom George This is a typical Formby situation comedy very much in the style of earlier Formby films - a kind of *It's in the Air* for the Navy. It was directed and produced by Marcel Verney with Ben Henry as co-producer. Charles Williams was the conductor/arranger. Harry was given 10 days to complete his contribution to the score.[101]

The plot concerns Navy club steward George who because of a low medical grade is turned down by the navy. Yet, he gets in by mistake when a sailor friend borrows his only suit of clothes and he is obliged to wear the sailor's uniform. Following a case of mistaken identity, he becomes involved with enemy agents based in a taxidermist's shop, and foils their attempts to blow up a British warship. Songs with words by Phil Park *Swim Little Fish, If I Had A Girl Like You, Bell Bottom George.*

---

[101] Bret, David, 1999, George Formby, Robson Books Ltd p. 129 (he gets the name of the forces band wrong!)

This latter is the usual strophic song for George the introduction based on the 'sailors hornpipe', the verse not quite as sharp as those provided earlier for him by Haine and Harper) but ending of each verse having the title repeated. The recording having the inevitable banjolele solo.

The Rest is Silence This was a play by Harold Purcell, staged for the first time on 20 April featuring Ann Todd, directed by David Lean. It was about the trial of Madeleine Smith, accused of poisoning her French lover with arsenic. Lawrence Olivier's talented cousin, Sheila Burrell made her debut as Rose in it on 20 April. It featured the song *We Shall Always Have Today* to words by Harold Purcell.

Jenny Jones. He became involved in writing the complete music for his next musical *Jenny Jones*[102] - another George Black promotion, due for the Autumn. He also wrote a couple of songs for films. Harry would be aware that D-Day was looming, being officially launched on 6 June. This meant that he had to get ready for possible future posting. He stayed in the *Sheriff's Private Hotel* in Bath on 10 June, possibly on the way to Swansea to see his family before embarking.[103]

He took part in a Band concert in Lewes Town Hall on 10. It provided a good illustration of the variety of music played at the time and what was in their repertoire, namely selections from popular operettas, musical comedies, their own band repertoire and items accompanying soloists whether instrumental or vocal.

It Happened One Sunday This was an ABPC film released on 28 July starring Robert Beatty, directed by Czech Karel Lumac, with Charles Williams as music director/ arranger.

Harry contributed 2 songs, a quasi-naval ditty, *All Ashore* and a more romantic number *Valley of Dreams* with a slight Irish nostalgic flavour nostalgia, as befits the heroine, an Irish servant girl Moya Malone (Barbara White). She is working in Liverpool and mistakenly believes that she has a secret admirer working at

---

[102] There is a handwritten copy in Parr-Davies collection.

[103] Bath Chronicle and Gazette

a hospital and while seeking him out accidentally meets and falls in love with a serviceman Tom Stephens (Canadian actor Robert Beatty. She spends the rest of the day going around Liverpool with him and they eventually decide to marry.

In N W Europe in the aftermath of War.

During the next month on 19 August, he got orders to go with the *Life Guard's Band* to the Western Front in France. Harry would now see much more of the effects of war than he did before with ENSA, not only as it affected military personnel, but ordinary people in different occupied countries. The musical efforts led by Captain Lemoine, which the Band made (including Harry) were more than mere morale-boosters for the forces and local people, but had a special significance in showing all they contacted that there was hope for the future.

The band initially moved from the eastern part of the D-Day Landings inland to Calvados in the Bocage south and west of Caen (once relieved of German occupation by the end of July) travelling mainly to villages and townships. The tour had initially mild autumn weather, which began to cool off in late September and through October. November brought even cooler clearer weather. Eventually this changed to more and more cloud until snow and frost appeared in December, a harbinger of increasingly severe winter weather in early January 1945 It did thaw afterwards. The tour was extensive, (one newspaper stated an unlikely 25000 miles) but logistically the tour left a lot to be desired as will emerge below.[104]

Harry was a long way from the comforts of Gracie, her family, his own family or of an hotel in London. Colleague musician Norman Bearcroft left a record of the band's tour in his diary (quotations from him are in italics):-

21 August.... *the first step was a move to a camp near Gosport on the 21ˢᵗ. The following day the Band boarded an American tank landing craft, Ops Neptune, manned by British seamen. At 9 o'clock the craft was packed with tanks and lorries, the only passengers being The Life*

---

[104] Harry's army record laconically has:- *Embarked for NE Europe – 22.8.44*

Guards Band and the band of the 'Shiny Tenth' Hussars [Prince of Wales' Own].

22 *Six or seven hours later the craft moved a little way of Portsmouth, where it waited for the convoy to assemble by midnight, then mover off round the Isle of Wight.*

23 *Landing on Juno Beach Normandy at 6.45 pm* [where British and Canadian forces had disembarked on D-Day].... *the musicians' first task was to help with the loading of British casualties and German prisoners, while waiting for transport to St Aubin-sur Me*r.[nearby village 10 miles N of Caen][105] *The camp at St Aubin was a rest camp for soldiers from the front.*

26.... *t*he *Band moved to St. Germain du Crioult,* [about 25 miles W and S of Caen], *only to find they were not expected and had to sleep under hedges with only greatcoats for bedding.*

27 *The following day instruments were unpacked, oiled and later played in a concert, given in Condé-sur-Noireau* [a crossroad village on main road few miles E] *for the 'Guards Armoured Division'* [part of XXX Corps].

28..... *concerts were played at Galigne,and Vassy, before moving to Lande Patry* [all villages west of cross roads.]

31 [moving 10 miles SE] *Concerts at Tinchebray*

1 September.... *and St Clare Dehalauze* [further SE 10 miles]

2....*was spent travelling to* Flers [NE about 12 miles] *and very rough accommodation in a German barracks.*

3.... *a concert played in a local cinema.*

---

[105]   Lawn, George R, 1995, *Music in State Clothing the Story of the Kettledrummers, Trumpeters and the Band of the Life Guards,* Lee Cooper, p. 50 George Lawn uses musician Norman Bearcroft's diary, about what happened to the bandsmen. The author has corrected spelling of place names and used [] to add relevant detail including locations.

The band in the following week moved east about 75 miles to wooded Upper Normandy.

11 *to Morgny-la Pommeray* [NE of Rouen]

12 *for a concert at Notre Dame d'Isle* [nearby Village]

13 *A day of general cleaning up, change of clothing and a mobile bath...*

14/15/16 *concerts starting at Etrepagny* [further 30 miles SE], *then playing for civilians at Limerick* [about 40 miles cross-country] *to Limetz-Villez and St Pierre d'Autils and in the evening for the Royal Artillery at Bonniéres-sur-Seine* [nearby villages]

20 *A brief period of comparative luxury, spent in the Three Merchants Hotel* [timber-framed Hôtel des Trois Marchands} *in Les Andelys* [25 miles SE of Rouen]

22 *After playing for local civilians, the Band provided the music.... for a swank (i.e. inspection) parade of the Scots Guards, followed by a long journey to give a concert the same evening for the Grenadier Guards.*[106]

23 *spent entertaining at a local hospital*

24 *playing at a sports meeting.*

The band now made its way to Brussels, 250 miles to the NE. The city had been relieved a month before on 4 September.

3 October *Leaving Les Andelys, they arrived in Brussels to enjoy the Splendid Hotel* [in North Brussels].

5/6 *Broadcasting from a Belgian studio*

7 *Concert at the Théâtre Royal de la Monnaie.* [Brussels Opera Hose]

---

[106] Both were constituent Corps of the *Guards Armoured Division.*

The typical programme included ;-

> *Steps of Glory*
> *Orpheus in the Underworld*
> *Charm of the Waltz,*
> *The Chocolate Soldier*
> *Excerpts from 'Aida'*
> *and Five minutes with Cole Porter.*

Several more performances were given in Brussels before leaving at 12 midnight on 24 October. They were moved on where *During their short stay in Holland the Band lived under canvas, four or five miles from the front line which was the River Maas.* – near the so-called 'Battle of the Dykes' liberating towns south of Maas.

> **25** *arrived at 8.30 am.... concert for... Welsh Guards.... at the Divisional Club*[107] [108]

> **26** *The Band played for their own regiment*

> **27** *concert.... for the Grenadiers*

> **28** *return to Brussels*

> **29** *to take the Royal Corps of Signals to church.*

> **4 November**.... *the Band now known as 'Monty's Pets', played for him at a dinner he gave for all the senior officers who had taken part at the Battle of El Alamein.*

> **8** *concert given at the Ancien Belgique* [large Brussels concert hall]

> **9** *rehearsals began for a parade on 11ᵗʰ at the Palais de Beaux Arts finished 2 in the morning;*

> **10** *this was followed later in day with another, then a performance in the evening*

---

[107]   Another constituent Corps of the *Guards Armoured Division.*

[108]   War diary 1ˢᵗ Battalion of Welsh Guards for 25 October 1944.

11 *concert in the presence of Her Majesty Queen Mary the Queen Mother.*

13.... *a concert given at Renaix* [40 miles W, close to French border]

14.... *the band said goodbye to the people of Brussels and moved to Tessenderloo* [50 miles E of Brussels]. *There the accommodation was a disused house, very dirty and no beds.*

17.... *on the road for Asse with a Corporal Major detailed as navigator, but Captain Lemoine insisted that he was in charge and would therefore navigate. Some hours later the Musicians were asking why all the road and shop signs were in German.*

They had moved steadily east into Germany! rather than NW towards Asse. After this there was 100 miles SW journey to a strip of Holland between the Belgian and German borders close to Maastricht:-

18 *to Geleen* [coal mining town] *to live in a theatre.*

19 *Church parade on Sunday*

20/21/22/23/24/25 *concerts played every day.*

Although there were grumbles from the Band, the comments also reveal the hardships of the local people, especially as the weather was getting colder:-

26 *to Brunnsum* [a few miles SW of Geleen] *The trip was so badly organised that they had done only about quarter of the playing they might have done.... They were billeted with civilians..... e.g. a back* kitchen with a stone floor.... *There was nothing to eat and the toilet facilities were down the garden*

27 - 30 November/1/2 December in area *including eating in a café 2 miles away, playing in a cinema 6 miles away and having a bath down a coal mine.*

3 *concert in Hoensbrock* [a few miles S near Hasselt]. They travelled all the way back to Asse.

5 *played for the 2ⁿᵈ Household Cavalry Regiment*

9 *played again or the 2ⁿᵈ Household Cavalry Regiment at Waterschei* [back to Hasselt area] *and afterwards slept on the floor as usual. More Concerts, inspections and prize-givings were undertaken in the next few days.*

15.... *dance band played for the US Air force on the night Glen Miller died.*

19 *A concert.... was cancelled five minutes before starting time, when the Regiment, as part of the Guards Armoured Division, were ordered up to assist the Americans at the Battle of the Bulge.*

25 December to 1 January *completely free. A concert in a Casino in Belgium started the ball rolling again.*

Despite the weather, they now moved back into Holland about 90 miles NE.

8.... *to snowy Eindhoven into civilian digs and concerts given in the local hospital and theatre. Nijmegen* [50 miles NE on German border] *was the next stop, living in a hospital, then a brief period of leave in Brussels.*

There is a lull in the account during the early weeks of the New Year and the Band returned to England on 9 March.[109]

Jenny Jones *Jenny Jones* was another George Black promotion. Harry must have written all the music from March to August, before he went off to Europe. The lyrics were again by Harold Purcell and scenario by Ronald Gow (author of the famous play *Love On The Dole*). He based it on short stories about South Wales coalfield by the Welsh poet Rhys Davies. The result was quite episodic e.g. in 2 acts and 12 scenes:-

Act 1	Scene 1	Morgan Jones Cottage
	Scene 2	The Ice Cream Parlour

---

[109]   This date is confirmed in Harry's war record.

Scene 3	The Hill Above the Town
Scene 4	St Ceiriog's Abbey
Scene 5/6	A Village Street

Unlike the realistic set for *How green was my valley,* the show's scenery was criticised for not having sight of a coal mine or slag heap and being very clean-looking no coal-dust anywhere. Verisimilitude was not a requirement in a lavish production.

The plot tells of Morgan Jones, (Sidney Bland) a Welsh miner in Aberdowlais[110], a father of 18 children, who wanted to make them 21 in number and seeks to find a new wife. The first act opens in the family cottage with Penry who loves daughter Jenny (Carole Lynne) and Morgan's his young son David who sings *My Wish.* Morgan's children come in to sing Henry Purcell's *Nymphs and Shepherds.*

There is a *Capri Serenade,* a play featuring Ugolini, Marie, Dai and Jimmy. Light relief is provided by a Geordie miner Jimmy Armstrong (Jimmy James) and his mum who become involved with the family. Dilys and her lover Paul sing *Where the Blue Begins.* There is the usual ballet sequence derived from an Anatole France book *The Story of Saint Ceiriog,* (Tommy Linden) with the reliable Wendy Toye choreographing the spectacle. Morgan Jones marries and the finale of act 1 has Jenny leaving her lover Penry (Ronald Millar) to go to London.

Act 2	Scene 1	A Herbalist's Shop
	Scene 2	The Market Place
	Scene 3	A Dressing Room
	Scene 4	The Stage of the Theatre at Aberdowlais
	Scene 5	The Hill Above the Town
	Scene 6	Backstage of the Theatre at Aberdowlais.

Act 2 opens with more from the children and Dilys and Paul in *Merry Go Round.* Dilys, Jenny's sister and Paul sing another duet, *After All.* Jenny comes back with an operetta (this device of an operetta in a musical yet

---

[110] Is this a corruption for theatrical purposes of Aberdulais, near Neath?

again) called *An Episode in Havana*, It was an historical romance (derived from a Doris Leslie book, possibly *Royal William; the Story of a Democrat*). about the future King William IV, Lord Nelson and a Local Cuban girl. Jenny wants people locally to perform it put on at the Aberdowlais Theatre Royal (see Act 2 Scenes 3 4 6). During its playing, Ugolino (baritone Kurt Wagener) sings *Don Vasco Salano* and the chorus (Vincent Tildesley Mastersingers) sing *Annabella*. Dilys and Paul sing yet another duet *Yet Another Day* and after a dance David sings *Ar hyd y nos*. Girl acrobats *The Three Wallabies also* perform. The music for this typically lavish and spectacular Black production was orchestrated by Debroy Somers and played by the Cranbourn Light Symphony Orchestra conducted by Bobbie Howell.

It had a short pre-London tryout (once again at the *Brighton Hippodrome*) from 12 September. It did not appear to be cohering very well so some of the show met with disapproval. Ronald Miller the romantic lead in it helped to reshape before it opened at the *London Hippodrome* on 2 October.[111]

It had a modest success running for 153 performances, closing in December. Being in N W Europe, Harry was not on hand to deal with the show's music, so never saw it as a complete entity. Indeed four numbers by Harry to words by Phil Park were brought in from the review, *Top of the World* (which had been bombed out 4 days after its London first performance in 1940).

The musical director was Bobby Howell. The costumes were designed by Norman Hartnell and Digby Morton. *The Observer* sniped that the Welsh episodes were as much like the real thing as the Rhondda is to Leicester Square. However, it ran for 153 performances.

Disagreement

Gracie and he not only cooperated musically over the years since 1932 on many enterprises even if they argued over details. Harry could be touchy if he felt he was not being properly acknowledged (as was seen in

---

[111] He went became speechwriter for Margaret Thatcher and creator of her famous catchphrase *The lady is not for turning.*

Canada). Both were compulsive workers. Gracie despite her considerable charm was quite a driven character. Until she met Monty, her emotional life was often quite subject to a fling with the man of the moment. Harry a mere observer during the years was more of a younger brother when he lived in Gracie's household.

Sadly in May 1945, things came to a head. Disagreeing with Gracie and her wish for him to accompany him on a tour to Australia and the Far East, Harry baulked and decided he not want to do war work anymore - claiming that he had seen enough of uniforms whilst he was doing military service to last him a life time. Misreading the intentions behind his words, later Gracie wrote to her sister rather cynically about the break-up being financial, *Harry – didn't mind going to Australia, but he wanted a nice remuneration in American dollars, which of course we couldn't afford. The upshot was that he did not go to Australia and finally accompanied Gracie no more.*

The situation was more complicated that either made out. Harry had responsibilities to the Life Guards Band as well as his West End commissions from August 1941 onwards. He had written on 4 major musicals, 10 songs for 2 revues and 13 songs for 9 films. He sometimes went beyond hid mental and physical resources trying to do too much and exhausted himself e.g. at the end of 1943. This possibly arose most likely due to stress of working in 2 different and opposing but demanding settings. The band was to take part on 6 June in the Victory parade in Paris. *The busiest section of the Band at this time was undoubtedly the dance band, celebration dances being a regular excuse for good times.*[112] In addition Harry had recently returned from an exhausting tour of duty in NW Europe for 8 months, which must have pushed him well out of every 'comfort zone' he had previously experienced - physical mental and social. He had viewed at first hand all the horrific after-effects of total war.

Before the Paris parade, te band had a concert in Cheltenham in early August in the offing, where he was to be featured with the band as soloist during a *Cheltenham Festival*. Following that, the Band was off again to Europe, this time for the Victory parades in Paris. Last but not necessarily

---

[112]   Lawn, George R, 1995, *Music in State Clothing the Story of the Kettledrummers, Trumpeters and the Band of the Life Guards,* Lee Cooper, p. 55

least, he had 2 songs to get ready for a Tom Arnold revue *Fine Feathers* mounted for Jack Buchanan to be premièred in London in October.

Despite this breach between them in fact the pair continued to communicate after they had returned from their respective tour of duty. She continued to sing his songs and the pair appeared occasionally together and Gracie's letters to him remained warm.

Cheltenham

Harry appeared again as a soloist in the Festival. The music provided by the band was part of a whole group of wide ranging activities – dog and horses shows, cricket and tennis matches, water polo, rambling, swimming, wrestling at a Sports festival in Cheltenham, held as before in early August. Beginning on 4 August for the week it ended on following Sunday.

The music provided included recitals by Louis Kentner the distinguished pianist, the Spa Orchestra and *The Band of His Majesty's Lifeguards* under Lieutenant-Colonel Albert Lemoine with a number of band members playing solos. On Saturday at the inaugural concert was held in Montpellier Gardens on 4 August. The band's extensive programme was:-

Offenbach - overture *to Orpheus in the Underworld*

Selections of music *by Ewing, Lehar, Debussy and Friedman*

Agostine (Three Trumpeters (with Musicians B J Clarke, Harry B Dunsmore and L-Corporal E D Mirams)

Debussy - Clair de Lune and

Richard Addinsell - The Warsaw Concerto (both with Harry).

Solo items by Dennis Macmanson (violinist originally from London Symphony Orchestra)

These soloists featured in the evening:-

Demarare - Cleopatra (Harry B Dunsmore (cornet))

Henry Bishop - Lo! Hear the gentle Lark (L-Corporal L Hazel and Corporal R G Thornburrow (flutes))

Geldard – 'Twixt Heather and Sea (Musician W Connor (xylophone))

Further selection were from *Sullivan's Iolanthe, Friedmann's* or *Dvorak's Slavonic Rhapsody No. 2, Wagner, Tchaikovsky, Raprecht* and *Monti*

Harry appeared with them playing the solo piano part in Richard Addinsell's popular wartime piece. The newspaper article is not clear but he no doubt repeated his solo 'spots' at the afternoon concerts on the Sunday and during the rest of the week.[113]

To Paris The band was given orders issued on 14 August to cross over to Paris. Harry embarked with them on 20 August. They were present on 25 August for the anniversary parade, commemorating France's liberation from the Nazi occupation. They returned on 1 September.

Fine Feathers A Tom Arnold revue this was devised by Robert Nesbitt starring veteran Jack Buchanan with experienced dancer/actress Ethel Revnell, exotic dancer Marqueez and experienced character actor 'Duggie' Wakefield. It had 2 acts with 8 individual sections each. There were a number of writers and composers. The doyen was Vivian Ellis, Ethel Revnell wrote a song she sang herself, despite taking a diversity of roles in many of the sections. Phil Park furnished not only lyrics for the four songs Harry penned, but wrote 2 songs one to his own lyrics and another to words by Alan Melville.

> Harry wrote the song incorporating the show's title, *Fine Feathers Make Fine Birds* setting a scene linking and aviary and fashion house. For the finale of Act 1, Harry provided Jack Buchanan with a deep South number to one of Park's best lyrics. It mimics a deep south minstrelsy number.

The orchestra was again conducted by Bobbie Howell with musical arrangements were by George Melachrino. It was staged on 11 October 1945 at the *Prince of Wales* and ran for 578 performances.

---

[113] 3 and 6 August 1945 Gloucestershire Echo

Chapter 13

DEMOBILISED (1946-9)

The Lisbon Story – the Film

There was a British National Film version of his 1943 musical *The Lisbon Story*. Retaining many of the original stage cast, the film displays fundamental changes in the presentation of the story line. It becomes more of an anti-Nazi thriller with a lot of extra expository scenes and dialogue to little real effect and strips a lot of its music in two ways. It cuts it out or puts it out of original context. It thus dissipates the tension accumulated especially in the second act of the musical. Patricia Burke becomes more decorative and prettily vocal than in the musical where she has a key role musically and dramatically. This is removed and her music is made into set numbers, not integrated into the story, through appropriate music and the use of melos. The *rive gauche* flavour at the beginning goes and melos and the ballet sequences are much reduced to one dance. At the end, Gabrielle is spared the assassin's bullet, her accompanist is shot instead!

There was a guest appearance by Richard Tauber singing *Pedro the Fisherman*. He does this well enough but without the life the original chorus had given the number. Harry provided a new song for Patricia Burke a pleasant set number *Paris in My Heart*. The musical director of the film was fellow-composer/conductor Hans May and orchestral arrangements were done out by Wilfrid Burns. Released on 21 February 1946, it was only a limited success as a film.

Now Harry became involved with 2 further revues on the cusp of being discharged from the Army.

High Time! This Val Parnell revue opened on 20 April at the Palladium. It featured a many popular stars of the time, especially Tessie O'Shea in her first review and regular Polish dance duo Alicja Halama and Ciesław Konarski. Harry only contributed to no 7 on the programme -*Yukon Nights - Down the Trail*, to words by Dick Hurran. The orchestra was the RAF band *The Sky Rockets* conducted by Paul Fenoulhet and he was responsible for the musical arrangements.

'Demobbed'

Papers were prepared from 9 April to release Trooper Harry Parr Davies 295736 quaintly given as being 'Musical Adviser to Associated British Picture Corporation Ltd' – a partial truth. He was 'demobbed' officially by Captain Gordon on 18 May 1946 from *His Majesty's Life Guards*.[114] He moved to his own mews flat at 11 Harriet Walk in nearby Knightsbridge. It would be chosen to give access to London's theatre land and to some more of his usual social contacts. He got ready 7 items and ballet music for a revue.

The Shephard Show This 2 Act revue subtitles *A Medley of Mirth and Music* opened on 26 September at the Princes Theatre. It had 8 numbers in each act. It featured 4 talented comedians, Eddie Gray (one of the original *Crazy Gang,* now solo), Richard Hearne (character actor), Arthur Riscoe (also a singer) and Douglas Byng (female impersonation as scene 2 *Madame Touchée).* Harry was as usual one of several providers of the necessary music as were John Blore (who conducted BBC Orchestra) and Michael Treford. Harry teamed up again with Harold Purcell.

---

[114] Household Cavalry Archive records 1946 for Harry Parr-Davies

They gave scene 4 *Mary Must Have Music;* No 5 *Passports for Two* for Marie Burke and bass singer Gavin Gordon; No 7 *Disconcerto* for singers and dancers including Marie Burke, Jeanne Ravel and others. In Act II, he went on to do the three final numbers 14 15 and 16. 14 *A song and a Story* is for comedian singer Arthur Riscoe; 15 looked like a ballet with vocals, *Chanson de Paris* (as Wendy Toye the experienced choreographer was involved) and *Bubbling Over* ended the show.

> The programme includes 3 pieces published as sheet music, *It All Comes Back To Me Now* (possibly from No.7); *Counting Sheep.* This is a deceptively simple, but charming song in Harry's accomplished nursery rhyme vein, about love stopping the singer going to sleep, after repeat of the refrain, he doses (z-z-z-z-)and piece ends quietly and *I Shall Always Remember.* This revue turned out to be the last revue with which Harry was involved.

Harry's career once he was demobbed showed a slowing up of musical activity. He wrote a few songs again published during 1947 and 1948, but without apparent connection with stage or film. There was *Annette, Angela Mia,* and two others of contrasting content and atmosphere, *Glen Echo* and *Peter the Penguin* and the Hollywood-ish theme song for *Maytime in Mayfair.*

Glen Echo reminiscent of Andy Stewart songs is competent, purporting to be Celtic or Scottish. The melody is typically Harry's i.e pleasantly enough worked out. Its introduction is the nearest he gets to a 'Celtic' flavour with its slightly eerie figure and harmony. The verse and refrain are much blander. The only Scottish feature is 'ye' in the lyric. The best feature is the gentle 'echo' effect in the accompaniment after the words of the title are sung. As usual, it is a vehicle for the singer to make effective.

> The other song *Peter the Penguin* is an almost Mahlerian lament for past using a three part nursery rhyme structure. The first part is about Peter love for his lady bird, and her rejection of him leading to his passing away. The middle is the reaction of his friends in the zoo, with an ironic return to the first tune as a summary.

There is some indication that Harry was suffering from a gastric ulcer which caused him to go to see his local GP in 1950. The causes for this can only be conjectured. Smoking was an ingrained habit. He became a member of the Savage Club and also had a small circle of friends. including lyricist Barry Thomas, Harold Purcell and later Christopher Hassall. How much they (and he) drank there is of course uncertain. His GP certainly warned him at this time not to have alcohol.

Lastly to add to the above, the effect the Band tour after D-day had could well have played its part. He had been protected from the harshness of social and military reality throughout his life until then. Reasonably well off financially, his family in Wales gave him the warmth of their support and the comforts of home life. Gracie her family and ménage had continued to give a similar sense of security, plus of course a sound start in his career during the 1930's. During the early part of the war, he had moved in sheltered circles in hotels with ENSA and with the Guards.

The conditions in NW Europe were very different. Accommodation was frequently rough, the people he saw were coming to terms with the aftermath of a German retreat, as told in the diary above. All of this must have had a profound effect on him. His 'demob' thrust him back like many another into 'civvy' life without much psychological preparation for the change.

The Savage Club

He was recorded in 1947[115] as being a member of the *Savage Club*, then situated at Carlton House Terrace.[116] This exclusive club was founded in 1857 and was named after Dr Samuel Johnson fey friend Richard Savage and has remained a gentleman's club for those belonging to the public professions i.e. connected with Art, Drama, Music, Literature, Science and Law and are acceptable to the their fellow 'Brother Savages'. When Harry was a member, it included members of the Crazy Gang, Arthur Askey, Webster Booth, Charlie Chaplin and HRH the Duke of Edinburgh. It has a fortnightly dinner and as well as obtaining daily meals and other forms of refreshment, members could be called on to

---

[115] Who Was Who 1947

[116] Now at 1 Whitehall Place

entertain fellow guests – it all sounds an arrangement very suitable for Harry.

He had picked up his friendship with Gracie sufficiently for them to come together for a Royal Command Performance performing for King George VI and Queen Elizabeth on 3 November 1947 at the Palladium Theatre. It was his family back in Swansea who provided him with the warm and security he needed..'Billie' was particularly close to him, always having his favourite 'treat', a Custard Slice' ready for him to tuck into when he came back to Swansea.

Her Excellency In preparation for a spring 1949 première, he worked with Manning Sherwin on a new musical. It did not have in reality a lot of music. It was more a series of comic situation for Cecily Courtneidge's talents. It was a kind of British precursor to Irving Berlin's very successful Ethel Merman vehicle, *Call Me Madam,* even as far as the sub-plots. The book was by Archie Menzies and Harold Purcell who also provided the lyrics.

Her Excellency Lady Frances Maxwell is the first lady British Ambassador to the South American Republic of San Barcellos. Act I deals with her reception at the hotel she is staying at there. She pursues getting a meat import contract for Britain in return exporting British pianos. The contract is to be obtained from Señor Riazza 'the Meat King' (Austin Trevor) in preference to negotiations by Martin Nash (Patrick Barr), the American Ambassador. On a personal level, she appears to favour each of these 2 men initially.

A double secondary love interest occurs when Jimmy Denham, (young Thorley Walters) the British commercial attaché is pursued by Margaretta Riazza, (Sandra Martin) the Meat King's daughter who eventually falls for Bill (John Probert) a Texan cowboy. This leaves Jimmy free to woo Mary Ccresset (Margaret Mc Grath), the embassy secretary. Musicals like this need plenty of incident. Billy Dainty, an experienced comic singer and dancer plays a puzzled toreador with a song *Steak and Samba.* He is subdued by the redoutable Frances.

Of the 7 musical numbers, there were 2 for Jimmy and a duet for Frances and Jimmy, Harry wrote only one of Frances' numbers *Sunday*

Morning in England, a quasi-nostalgic number for Courtneidge to include her comic character impressions of folk back home. It was the best remembered song of the show. There was also *I Wonder* and *Diplomacy*.

After the usual provincial try-out of 2 weeks in each place, the show started on 19 April at the Alhambra Glasgow, followed by Birmingham, Nottingham, Southsea and Brighton, where it closed on 11 June. Its London première was on 22 June at London Hippodrome was not well received and only became a success later, running for 252 performances. There was critical and audience acclaim for Courtneidge's comic versatility and Harry's number for her gained the most plaudits.

Maytime in Mayfair He became involved with an Anna Neagle musical, *Maytime in Mayfair*. It features suave penniless man- about-town Michael Gore-Brown (Michael Wilding who has inherited a dress salon whose chief designer is Eileen Grahame (Anna Neagle) They decide to make it work, but are hindered by rival D'Arcy Davenport (Peter Graves) who fancies Eileen. Character actor Nicholas Phipps plays Sir Henry Hazelrigg, Gore-Brown's cousin, a clubland military bore but who is betraying the fashion secrets to Gore-Brown's rival. There is much Astaire-and Rogers dancing from Neagle and Wilding on the way to all ending happily.

> Harry is called only to provide the title song, a fairly typical lushly scored ballad song of the period. For these two enterprises Harry wrote fit-for-purpose music – pleasant and well crafted - but lacking some of his previous pulse and originality.

He took part in a broadcast of 'Welsh Rarebit' in a BBC Radio Light Programme Broadcast from Cardiff, dedicated to him in a short interview and airing some of his music. As his two current shows were being featured, i.e. in mid-summer 1949 title song *Maytime in Mayfair* was given a lavish choral backing, male and female soloists, a full orchestra with Harry playing the piano as part of the backing. *Pedro the Fisherman* was given an airing also.

Harry after this comparatively fallow period suddenly moved into a higher gear in 1950 with similar creative energy to 1943, 1944 and earlier restored and matured and fully in evidence.

Chapter 14

MORE MUSICALS (1950-51)

Dear Miss Phoebe

Dear Miss Phoebe had lyrics by Christopher Hassall who had served Ivor Novello so long and well with memorable verses. This was an adaptation of Sir *James* Matthew *Barrie's Quality Street* (1901), with much of the original dialogue in place. otherwise it was separated by appropriate musical numbers, some developed from ideas in the play's dialogue.

Eric Coates had set some of Hassall's verses in 1938. Knowing Coates was searching for material to set as a musical, Hassall had later offered Coates to set his version of Barrie's play as a musical.[117] In the event, Harry took up Hassall's skilful re-ordering of the play. Aiding in setting the show up were director Charles Hickman and Doris Zinkeisen with costumes and scenery.

---

[117] Self, Geoffrey, 1986, *In Town Tonight,- a centenary study of the life and music of Eric Coates,* Thames Publishing, p.88

Harry responds to this with a more refined, less exuberant score. It is nearer an Edward German model of musical comedy/operetta than previously, using waltzes, marches and period ballet music. Being closely based on a play makes it feel more integrated than other musicals he had written. To give the dialogue point, much of it is underpinned with key melodies played either before they appear or in reminiscence of them, revealing often what is going in the character's mind. The story is set during Napoleonic war (1805) in gossipy Quality Street, where Phoebe and Susan Throssel live. Young doctor Valentine Brown *(Peter Graves) has met 20 year old* Phoebe Throssel, *(Carol Raye) on several previous occasions and they like each other.*[118]

The overture (No.1) is a mixture of the main melodies. It leads to a minuet being played on a harpsichord as the curtain rises on a blue and white drawing room with a vie w through a wide window giving on to the street. The Throssel sisters' friends, Fanny and Mary Willoughby and Henrietta Turnbull are there with Susan. Fanny is reading from a thrillingly romantic novel, about which the orchestra comments. After more gossip during the introduction to next number (No.2), set to a slow, but regular gallop during which Phoebe comes in. She goes on to relate in her song, (arranged from the original dialogue), how when out shopping she met *A Certain Individual.* Susan interjects short comments and exclamations. It was Valentine, who is coming to see her this very afternoon.

Reilly the Irish recruiting sergeant for the Infantry (or Redcoats) (baritone Bernard Clifton) now enters. Phoebe and he exchange banter. He says he has a new recruit. Using a line from act II of the play, Hassall inserts a drinking song in the form of a duet, (No. 3) *Cowslip Wine* he toasts a local barmaid, she the fighting men, she eventually shows him the door to a postlude based on the song's main melody. It is a rollicking song in the tradition of *Porterlied* sung by Lionel in Flotow's *Martha.*

Susan, who had prepared a wedding dress in a blighted hope of getting married,- offers it to Phoebe, who now enters a reverie about love (No.4), a charming waltz song, *I'm Living A Dream.* Valentine now calls. He tells

---

[118] like Gabrielle in Lisbon Story this role requires a lyric soprano with a good top register

Phoebe much to her disappointment that he has enlisted, (the one the sergeant had mentioned). After a flourish on the harpsichord he tells her that (No. 5), *I Leave my Heart in an English Garden*. She is the garden he leaves behind (again Hassall develops a short paragraph in the play into the musical's best known number. Verse I tells about what Valentine likes about the garden, but verse II reveals that he has done the Grand Tour of Europe. Phoebe joins him and the piece ends as a duet. Susan learns of the result of the meeting with a reprise of *I Leave* as a melos under the dialogue. Phoebe weeps with disappointment.

Here Hassall adds a very effective scene to the original play. A reveille sounds as the scene changes to the street outside and Reilly reads a proclamation over military music (No.7). This is followed by (No.8) *March of the Redcoats*[119] a lively quick march. Reilly sings of the people he has enlisted the men join him in chorus and then tells them what they will experience in war. The ladies of the chorus join in to bring the scene to a triumphant close.

Scene three occurs ten years later (1815) in the same room but changed into a school room. The soldiers' march is briefly heard (No.9) before moving into the children's ballet (No. 10). This refashions and amplifies the school part in the original. The children are assembling. It starts with a Skipping Theme and using the ropes as reins, is transformed into Horse Theme ballet, the Throssel's outspoken maid Patty (Gretchen Franklin) bustles in. There is a knock and she rushes to open the door. Some more boys enter to a gallop – a variant of later Act II song (No.24) *I Can't Resist the Music*. Another knock and the girls come in shyly to a jumpy variant of another act II song *When will You Mary Me* (No.22). The tune becomes more flowing as they become bolder. A boy plays 'Chopsticks' on the harpsichord, then the Blackboard Theme a snatch of *Cowslip Wine* followed by drawing a cat on the board. Phoebe in plain clothes and with straight hair starts a French lesson, *Après vous*, Susan similarly dressed enters and the children practise the minuet (heard at the curtain rise of Act I). An Algebra lesson occurs, the music of the melos shows Phoebe thinking of the evenings Waterloo Ball by anticipating its waltz song *Whisper While You Waltz*. This continues through the Latin lesson.

---

[119]   The sheet music erroneously gives the soldier on the right side of the cover a blue uniform!

To the tune of *I Leave My Heart* (No. 13) Valentine (now a Captain) comes in. He has lost his left hand. Phoebe and he converse awkwardly. When he has gone, Phoebe and Susan discuss the situation to the background music of (No.14) *Whisper While You Waltz* and *I'm Living A Dream*. She sees herself as too old for romance. Susan remains and the orchestra plays the beadle's night watch song *All's Well To-night*. (No.15). Patty now confesses to Susan that she would loves to have a lover in a song with a jig-like rhythm. (No.16) *The Love of a Lass*.

Phoebe sings a short reprise of *I'm Living A Dream*. (No.17) and now decides on her plan. She will outwit and partly avenge herself on Valentine by appearing as 'Livvy' her own (fictitious) niece dressed in the old bridal gown of Susan's and with ringlets to make her look younger when she goes to the ball. The music under the dialogue continues her reprise and then turns (No.18) to *Whisper While You Waltz* as she thinks about the ball. Valentine comes in and is courteous to, but not deceived by 'Livvy' and together they sing and dance (No.19), Whisper While You Waltz, the chorus joining in to provide a climax and curtain call.

There is an intermission based on this latter tune (No. 20) before the curtain goes up to reveal the ball room. Charlotte, loved by Blades and Spicer, both ex-pupil soldiers, Patty and the ladies of the chorus in Wallflowers, bemoan the way men behave to women. The next number puts the lie to this as Patty collars Reilly and asks him (not coyly) *When Will You Marry Me and Carry Home*, a tune to a steady gallop. He replies to her reluctantly at first, but gets caught up with her insistent liveliness.

The situation changes to 'Livvy' and her flirting with Ensign Blades and Lieutenant Spicer in a light hearted skittish trio, *I Can't Resist the Music*. (No.24) discussing how 'Livvy' can't resist dancing with a number of beaux. The other men in the chorus join in.

Valentine enters and 'Livvy' and discusses the meaning of love, obliquely outlining their love for each other. He breaks out with a reprise (No.25) of *I Leave My Heart*, now recast as 'I Found My Love' not for 'Livvy', but the real Phoebe.

Hassall adds another scene at this stage not in the play. The beadle as a kind of night watchman tries to make sure the young bucks all get off home. Harry writes one of his most haunting melodies, *All's Well Tonight* (No. 26) under the dialogue already heard briefly in the ballet music. There follows a numbers of reprises (No.27) as the men of the chorus sing the recruitment song of act I, the whole chorus sing (yet again) *Living a Dream, Whisper While You Waltz, and I Leave My Heart* finishing the scene in a climax.. This is presumably so the audience will become even more familiar with the music - a kind of contemporary plugging!

All's Well Tonight (No. 28) is now vocalised by the beadle and harmonised chorus at the end of which they slowly disperse. The gossipy friends, Fanny, Mary and Henrietta not realising Phoebe's trick has been unmasked tell about *Livvy Is Having One of Her Turns* (No.30) to a slow gallop. This allows the scene to be changed back to the Throssel's front room where a charming ballad is sung *Spring Will Sing a Song*, (No.31) first by Phoebe and then taken up as a duet with chorus by her and Valentine. Strangely the dialogue supervenes in the final section, with *I Leave My Heart* being played by the orchestra.

Despite the overplaying at time of some of the numbers, this is the most satisfying complete of Harry''s musicals and with *The Lisbon Story* demonstrates his skills with a viable genre of theatre. His melodies, the musical characterisation and context as provided for him are consistently worked out.

The musical first opened at the *Theatre Royal*, Birmingham under Emile Littler on 31 July 1950, followed by 2 nights in Bournemouth, then at Swindon, Folkestone, Southsea and Oxford until 30 September when it opened a London run at the *Phoenix Theatre* on 13 October 1950, running for 283 performances until 16 June 1951.

Tired of the one way traffic of musical into London from USA, a group of theatre managers composers and writers formed an association to push British musical in other countries, particularly America. Among those concerned were Messrs Emile Litttler, Guy Bolton, Harold Purcell, Harry Parr Davies and Christopher Hassall It was 20 years, i.e well before the war that a British musical, *Bitter Sweet* had been exported to the states. A musical based on Mendelssohn and Jenny Lind was being propared. A start was made with *Music at Midnight (His Majesty's Theatre)*. The opening was attended by theatre represntatives from Stockholm, Germany,

France – their version was nearly ready – and Lee Shubert's man from New York. Harry (and Christopher Hassall) must have been gratified that all were going to see *Dear Miss Phoebe* to test the possibilites there.[120] Unfortunately, it took other later composers to make an impression on the international msical scene. Harry's musicals, songs and revues have remained at best tied to the British stage only.

'Blue For A Boy or What shall we do with the Body?'

Harry's other 1950 musical (a musical romp) of 8 pieces in a show more like a loosely connected farcical revue, and really consequently much less demanding. Harold Purcell was the lyricist in what was to be the last musical they did together. Its source was a German comedy *Hurrah! Eine Junge!* by Franz Arnold and Ernest Bach. There had been an English version in 1930 originally directed by Austin Melford, who again directed and played a comic role in this new piece. Emile Littler was again the manager.

The piece was written to exploit the cigar-smoking, rotund comedy star Fred Emney, dressed in blue baby rompers. It is set in the Bompard's villa in Deauville. He played gambler Fred Piper the mischievous loud and large stepson (dressed in a blue huge romper suit) of Dudley Leake (Austin Melford). He wants to keep the existence of Fred a secret. Dudley is to celebrate the first anniversary of his remarriage to lovely Mary Leake (Hermene French). Hercule (Guy Fane) and Emily Bompard (Bertha Belmore) are her parents. She and the female chorus open the musical with *A Year Ago Today*. Visiting guest lady novelist Anita Gunn (Eve Lister) joins them to sing the title song *Blue for a Boy*. This is in Harry's quasi-nursery rhyme vein Emily appears (she is eager to see her grandson) and joins Anita and Mary, *You've Got Him where You Want Him* to close act 1.

Fred has chosen to make himself known to his stepfather's new wife. Mary with the girls, which Fred loves to have round him sings *I Fancy My Chances*. Fred is aided in his pranks by the unlikely named solicitor

---

[120] Evening Telegraph Perth 13 November 1950. This initiative could well have come from the Songwriters Guild of Great Britain. Their annual concerts started in 1950 and went on until 1964 usually being held in 2nd week of March (see Chronology)

Dickie Skippett (young comedian, Richard Hearne). Fred and Caprice sing *A Little Bit on Account* and Anita sings *At Last It's Happened*; a song about not believing love can happen and then realising it has. This is followed by Anita singing the very beguiling *Lying Awake and Dreaming* another of Harry's numbers about loving and dreaming. It starts off with the emptiness of a house at night, then the refrain recounts how yearning can affect sleeping or not. This leads to a dance by eight chorus girls and a male principal dancer (Terence Theobald). They all work through various farcical predicaments, where even Fred and Dudley each takes off the lady novelist in drag i.e. Anita. After a reprise of *At Last It's Happened,* there is a finale. There are some peculiarities in the show e.g. no male chorus and a division between the farcical and the romantic mainly through Harry's songs for Eve Lister hardly nd integrated show, but it did well.

Following opening at the *Theatre Royal,* Birmingham, it underwent the further adjustments, before a 16 week preliminary to London tour. It went to Bournemouth, Glasgow and Newcastle for 2 performances, and then on to Blackpool, 2 more performances in Liverpool, on then to Sheffield, Nottingham and 2 more in Manchester until 20 November. Its London opening at *His Majesty's Theatre* on 30 November and ran for 664 performances, closing 28 June 1952 before going off on a further provincial tour.

CHAPTER 15

FINAL YEARS (1951 - 1955)

In November 1950, there was a triumphant production by Neath Operatic Society of Lisbon Story in the previous November in Neath, This was followed by a warm hearted reception and a celebratory dinner given by the Mayor, his tutor's brother Parrott. This must have been an occasion of pride to the family and even some of his schoolteachers like Miss M T Harvey, his French teacher at the Grammar School. Harry replied to tributes from various members of the Council by commenting that A composer must have knowledge of Bach and Handel before he could himself write a tune, and it was Mr Perrott who had given him the courage to go on and try to get somewhere. Afterwards, he expressed his gratitude to Miss Harvey by writing out for her a poem by Goldsmith.

Sadly shortly after this on 23 January 1951, Harry's father died at 9 Lôn Cadog, the family home at Swansea. He was 71. He was interred in what was the family grave at Oystermouth cemetery on 29 January. The request for gentlemen only for the obsequies no doubt included Harry and 'Billie''s husband Geoffrey and the cousins from Pontypridd, who would attend Harry's funeral 4 years later. His father had helped Harry with his career by proudly sending regular pieces to the South Wales Evening Post over the years about the progress his son was making.

Harry still had a number of inter-related physical and mental strains which his father's death and seeing the scores launched for three major musicals in the West End and his cigarette smoking and intake of alcohol which Dr Patrick Warren his doctor advised not to have.[121]

> He wrote two songs which were published to words by Harold Purcell. He set *Lero-Lilli-Bull-Ero*, a march known for its many different word settings from the days of the Battle of the Boyne (1690). from Marlbrough's campaigns in early 1700's. It now becomes a celebration of the Festival of Britain in 1951 *The Song of the Festival Fires*. The verses talk about Britain in a lightly jingoist frame of mind in a simple and clear musical arrangement.

> The other song was a waltz for duo Anne Ziegler and Webster Booth, a more muted number than earlier *My Paradise,* Love stay in my heart. It is a pleasant if slightly dated Rombergian number, but suitable for the duo.

Glorious Days Anna Neagle won a popular audience for her *Coronation Year* romantic pageant *The Glorious Years*. It had a pre-season try-out in the closing years of 1952, at the *Empire Theatre Nicholson Street Edinburgh*. rather surprisingly considering its distinctly English flavour.

It featured rather contrived situations to showcase Anna Neagle's versatility. A young London actress (Anna Neagle), knocked unconscious by a bomb explosion during the blitz, who dreams she's *Nell Gwyn* and *Queen Victoria*, the inspiration for her own future. (Anna played Nell Gwyn and Queen Victoria again.)[122] Errol Flynn came from Hollywood to join Anna Neagle as her co-star: David Farrar played King Charles, in the Nell Gwyn episode, and Peter Graves Prince Albert (the male lead in *Dear Miss Phoebe* in 1950). In the cast list, Sean Connery again appeared

---

[121] Obituary in the 'Times' 1/11/1955

[122] She had already played Queen Victoria in the Wilcox film, *Sixty Glorious Years*

as an extra – a Guard in this first screen appearance.[2123] In the New Year 1953, it was staged at the *Palace Theatre* London from 28 February 1953. It lasted eight months. It had 4 songs characterful songs by Harry the title song, *Glorious Days*, the hyper patriotic *The Song of England* (sung by Lorraine Tunstall), *Up the Hill to Windsor Castle* and a lively pseudo folksy *Hop, Skip and Jigstep.*

> This number is a pleasant country dance creation in common time.. After a jaunty 8-bar jig, the voice enters (in mood like *Boys and Girls Come Out to Play)* with more provocative lyrics in a verse about a lady dancing in the town. This is followed by the usual refrain and a coda - and 8-bar jig repeated as a code. This leads to a repeat of verse, refrain 2 and another 8-bars of jig, leading to the 'envoi' of refrain 3 and final instrumental jig.

The show was later transferred to the screen with a miscellany of songs by Anna's husband the director, Herbert Wilcox as **Lilacs in the Spring.** The only song which survived from the original stage musical which Harry had written was *Up the Hill to Windsor Castle.*

Harry kept contact with Monty's family and took himself off to Italy for a holiday in September 1954. He sent a post card home on 24 September:-

Sat. Morning.

It is really wonderful. Hot sunshine and wonderful food. I've had a nice few days with Monty's brother and sister – nice people. The plane was one (unreadable) 2 hours and 45 mins. I am going to Sorrento tomorrow. I am going to the film studios tomorrow. I may get a film. B

Here Harry sounds quite full of life - touring Italy as Monty's family lived in Cesena, near Rimini and Ravenna in the north east of Italy and then off to recently refurbished Cinecittà, SE of Rome and before setting off to Sorrento (perhaps to go to Capri).

---

[123] Christopher Bray, 2010, *Sean Connery the Measure of the Man*, Faber and Faber, p 21

Harry also contributed the title song for *Associated British Picture Corporation* romantic Technicolor film *Now and Forever,* directed by Mario Zampi with a script by R E Delderfield, based on his play, *The Orchard Walls.* Here are two young lovers society girl Janette Grant ('coming of age' Janette Scott) and motor mechanic Mike Pritchard (Vernon Gray) are lovers, much to the disapproval of her father J Pritchard (Jack Warner) who stops her seeing Mike. She attempts suicide, decides to elope to Gretna Green in an MG midget. This sparks off a nation-wide hunt. There were many cameo roles, for Pamela Brown, Sonia Dresdel, Bryan Forbes, Moultre Kelsall, David Kossoff, Wilfrid Lawson, Michael Pertwee and Ronald Squire.

Music was provided by Stanley Black, but Harry wrote its title song, *Now and Forever,* which Janette Scott and Vernon Gray sing. It is a slow waltz song to simple lyrics by Christopher Hassall. It consists of an introduction and refrain which can be repeated, the sentiments being a pledge of long-lasting love - a neatly put together romantic ballad.

The film was released after his death in February 1956, although the title song was copyrighted and published in 1955, making it his last composition.

Final musicals

It was about this time, that he began to work on his next musical for Emile Littler, with Eric Maschwitz with whom he had worked in the past. It was to be an adaptation of [3] *Peg O' My Heart,* J Hartley Manner's 1912 play, popular on both sides of the Atlantic. Made into a radio play there were also both silent and 'talkie' film versions of it, notably for Marion Davies in 1937. Littler commented on the night after Harry died *I was negotiating with them to work with me on a musical version of Peg O' My Heart. We were going to call it 'Marry Me Margaret' We should have met last week to begin work. I had to call the meeting off. We should have met this week.. I consider this man a genius. One of the best composers in the business.*

The play concerned love, class and money. A penniless Irish girl Margaret O'Donnell is informed that she has inherited a £2 million bequest from the father-in-law of Pats deceased wife by a London lawyer, Sir Jerry Markham, Unknown to her a placement of 3 years, costing £5000 has been made for her to stay with Lady Chichester and her family. So, she has to leave her father Pat in Ireland who is reluctant to see her go, but is philosophical about it. She travels to England as part of the condition of inheriting a fortune. She witnesses and experiences much there. Eventually until she finds true love with Sir Jerry Markham, the lawyer who had originally brought the news of the legacy.

Harry had a limited social life[124] and had lived alone at 11 Harriet Walk, Chelsea[41][125] from 1950. While he was not particularly party or media conscious, he came to have a number of close friends arising from his collaborative work with his lyricists. As Christopher Hassall notes in his letter to his mother after his death:- *It was a happy relaxation to be in his company and my work with him was never a labour, always a joy.*[126]

During mid September In the weekly called 'Red Letter Days', Harry gave an interview/article about Gracie in which he recalled somewhat neutrally anecdotes about their working relationship.

The Inquest

Sadly, he died alone on October 14, 1955 in his house, only later being found dead by his domestic the next morning with a bowl beside him. His body was identified by his sister Marjorie, who had rushed to Knightsbridge once she read about it, not realising that his mother Rosina or sister Glenys didn't know.

The inquest on him appears to have been in at least two stages. It was opened on c 16 October and was adjourned until 31 October with the distinguished Hammersmith Coroner Major H Neville Stafford sending certain body fluids (in the bowl) for analysis to the police laboratory. The final verdict that Harry Parr-Davies, aged 41, composer and song writer, died from stomach haemorrhage, caused by acute alcoholic gastritis was recorded at the resumed inquest at Hammersmith on 31 October.[127] There

---

[124] According to Harry's sister, 'Billie' in www. billhanks.co.uk

[125] Rex Walford 2004, *Harry Parr Davies,* Oxford Dictionary of National Biography, p. 364

[126] Included in Hanks, www. billhanks.co.uk

[127] Obituary in the *Times,* 1/11/1955

was a certain irony at this time, if had lived he may well have appeared on 29 October in another Royal Command Performance at the Palladium, accompanying Gracie.

Harry had a lifelong fear of doctors nor did he heed medical advice about not having alcohol. Smoking at this time was not made so much of an issue but added physical, psychological and emotional stress were all factors associated with peptic ulceration. Possibly Even taking a small amount of alcohol could cause the ulcer to perforate, thus leading to internal haemorrhage and a subsequent fatal peritonitis. He would have had intense pain which would have prompted physical collapse prior to his death, a situation not made easier by being alone. It was a sad conclusion to a life dedicated to make people happier through his music.

The body was taken to Swansea, the funeral being held at Holy Trinity Church Sketty with the Rev H Wynne Griffiths, Vicar of Trinity performing the funeral rites according to the *Church of Wales*. Afterwards, he was interred at Oystermouth Cemetery at Mumble Head on the west of Swansea Bay in the family plot beside his father. The funeral was an occasion in which the remaining family participated as well as civic dignitaries. The cortege left from 9 Lôn Cadog Cwngwyn, Swansea, his parent's home for the last 20 years. His mother was chief mourner, accompanied by brother-in-law Geoffrey David; Leonard Howells of Port Talbot, William and Frederick Davies were cousins from his father's side of the family from Pontypridd; and F Hughes and H. Harrison possibly family friends were also there Local dignitaries present at the service were[128]:

> *Councillor C. Martin Davies, representing the Midland Bank Executor and Trustee Company;*
>
> *T.J.H. Griffiths manager of the Wind Street branch of the bank (for whom Harry's sister Glenys worked);*
>
> *From Swansea:- Councillor Hywel Thomas; J Barlow; T J Harries; J D Davies, manager of Barclays Bank, Uplands; A Bruce Davies,*

---

[128] As Davies is such a common name in the area it is difficult to know who are related, unless explicitly stated.

manager of Lloyds Bank, Uplands (Geoffrey Dqvid worked there so
had 'Billie' before she married;

*From Neath:- G W Knoyle; Derek Pratt; H S Williams; W G Davies;
F J Evett; F H Brooks; Owen Joseph; W J Barrett; Miss Joseph.*

Rev H Wynne Griffiths, Vicar of *Trinity Church, Sketty* performed the
funeral rites according to the *Church of Wales*. Floral wreaths were sent
by Gracie, *With deepest sympathy, Gracie Fields* and from *The Song-Writers
Guild of Great Britain,* 'in loving memory', directors and staff of Frances
Day and Hunter Ltd and from Fred and Doris Day. Probate showed that
he left £7633/14/10d.[129] Apart from £170 death duty, he left his mother
£500 and the rest of his estate was divide equally between his sisters.
However, 'Billie' later recalled that for years afterwards royalties still came
in. Christopher Hassall sent a letter to his mother.

My Dear Mrs Parr Davies,

> *Though we have not met, I feel very close to you at this time,
> through my sympathy for your grievous loss, which I deeply share. As
> you know Harry was an intimate and beloved friend of mine as well
> as a collaborator in my work. He was one of only two or three people
> I have ever loved with whom I was completely at ease. It was a happy
> relaxation to be in his company, and my work with him was never a
> labour always a joy. Work will never be such fun again.*

> *Within the last ten days (from c. 4 October), we had two of our
> happiest evenings together; one evening we went to see a musical
> play[130] at the Piccadilly Theatre and then went on the Ivy[131] for*

---

[129] Rex Walford 2004, *Harry Parr Davies,* Oxford Dictionary of National Biography,
p. 364 i.e. about £800000 by 2014 values

[130] This was very likely to have been *Romance in Candlelight.* The London show had
a good promising cast;- Sally Ann Howes, Jacques Pils, Patricia Burke, Roger
Dann, under the expert musical direction of Alexander Faris, but it lasted for a
mere 53 performances from 15 September 1955. The critics agreed with Harry
and Christopher Hassall. It was one of the unrevivable flops of 1955.

[131] The Ivy opened in 1917 is an exclusive restaurant on West Street, which has over
the years has catered for theatre goers and players.

supper. We both hated the play, which stimulated us into a lot of talk about how we could have done much better ourselves. Then another night he introduced me to his friend Basil Thomas (1912- 1955).

Gracie the next month sent a letter to Glenys, Harry's older sister:-

My Dear Glenys,

Thank you for your letter. I find it difficult to put into words my feelings, it's impossible to express this deep sorrow.

He was too young to leave us.

Harry's musical knowledge and imagination, and most perfect piano execution, made him one of the most outstanding pianists. When he was going through a spot of nervous tension, I was always happy to see him going home to you all he always came back more calm & happy to go on with his work.

I only wish we could have done more for him, poor boy was so mixed inside.

May the Good Lord give his soul Peace and contentment.

Always sincerely yours

Gracie

Harry's mother Rosina died on 29 March 1964, at 4 Broadway Sketty, Swansea. After Harry's death she must have moved to live with either one of her daughter's. She was buried with her husband and son in the joint family grave.

His younger sister, the one who worked for the Swansea branch of the *Midland Bank*, died in 1974 and her ashes were scattered over the family grave.

Marjorie David (or 'Billie' as she was called) lived on until 2011. She showed her deep affection for her brother Harry by providing much information often in the shape of anecdotes about him to Bill Hanks for his web site history and to George Lawn for his history of *His Majesty's Life*

Guards. As with her sister, her ashes were scattered on the family grave at Oystermouth.

Family Grave

Harry Parr Davies's sister, Billie David, unveiling the plaque to commemorate Harry at Neath Town Hall on the 24th May 2000

POSTSCRIPT

How to sum up Harry's achievements? There are two main aspects to his life- the personal and the musical.

In purely human terms, his life was short. Through a large part of early life as child and adult, he had been protected emotionally, first by his family who remained devoted to him and his career in music and by Gracie who saw him much as a talented younger brother. Even during the war, he had a comparatively sheltered existence, working the West End revue and musical scene. This continued even after his call-up.

The major factor that broke into his lifestyle was the earlier ENSA tour and even more so the August 1944 - March 1945 tour of relieved NW Europe after D-day. His health became poorer on his return to UK and despite rallies to produce musicals and songs ultimately didn't prevent the factors leading to his sudden death. His life was by and large centred arouud the music he made as part of the light entertainment establishment.

He was well-respected and humorous, a hard and generous almost obsessional worker at his craft, mildly ambitious and easily stressed. He was not a social being but had a few close friends besides his family.

His music within the light music genre has a surprisingly wide range from sentimental via the whimsical to the comicwith spme degree of restraint in its expression. He wrote his own lyrics throughout his life. They are at best charming if limited to conventional images from nature or from feelings of nostalgic love. They have little of Cole Porter's, Irving Berlin's or Lorenz Hart's wit being more akin to the British tradition of Horatio Nichols Vivian Ellis and Ivor Novello. The lyricists with which he collaborated especially Harold Purcell and Christopher Hassall gave him material well suited to his rather roman tic-tending abilities. Any piece by him is always well and carefully crafted. His songs weld words to music easily and to the best advantage for the singer.

There is throughout his output a stylistic movement too from the earlier jazz and music hall styles via a trend for operetta type waltzes, Latin American and Swing through to the more serious ballads often nostalgic of WW2 years until the more whitty expression of mood of the fifties and two late musicals. While not adventurous in choosing remote keys or extravagant harmonies, he moves easily and appropriately from major to minor. He supports the vocal line with varied harmonies, traditional sometimes, at others with mild jazz or chromatic sequences.

Although the resulting music can be at times be routine, especially if not stimulated sufficiently by the text or possibly overworked, generally Harry's responses to verses and refrain are deftly appropriate. In a large number of his songs, the melodies are memorable. Indeed some have passed into the nation's canon of favourites, others still await discovery as the investigation of light music of 20th century continues into the 21st.

APPENDIX 1

ALPHABETICAL LIST OF COMPOSITIONS

Songs

No.	Name	Type/source	Year
1	A Certain Individual	Musical - Dear Miss Phoebe	1950
2	After All	Musical - Jenny Jones	1944
3	All Ashore	Film - It Happened on Sunday	1944
4	All's Well Tonight	Musical - Dear Miss Phoebe	1950
5	Alone with You	Revue - Top of the World	1940
6	A Melody at Dawn	Film - This Week of Grace	1933
7	Anna from Anacapri	Film - Look Up and Laugh	1935
8	Angela Mia	Song	1948
9	Annabella	Musical - Jenny Jones	1944
10	Annette	Song	1948
11	April in the Spring of Love	Musical - Lisbon Story (tour)	1945
12	A Song and a Story	Revue - The Shephard Show	1946
13	A Song in Your Heart	Film - The Show Goes On	1935
14	As 'Round and 'Round We Go	Revue - Haw-Haw	1939
15	At Last It Happened	Musical - Blue for a Boy	1950
16	A Year Ago To-day	Musical - Blue for a Boy	1950

17	Baritone Song	Revue - Big Top	1942
18	Bell Bottom George	Film - Bell Bottom George	1944
19	Be Refined (cut)	Musical - Full Swing	1942
20	Best Bib and Tucker	Revue - Best Bib and Tucker	1942
21	Binkie's Lullaby	Film - Keep Your Seats Please	1936
22	Bird Cage Walk	Musical - The Glorious Years	1952
23	*Blue Bird of Happiness*	*Words only*	1935
24	Blue for a Boy	Musical - Blue for a Boy	1950
25	Bring Back the Girl in the Old-fashioned Gown	Song	1935
26	Bring in the Prisoner	Operetta – The Curfew	1927
27	Bubble, Bubble	Revue - Black Velvet	1940
28	Bubbling Over	Revue - The Shephard Show	1946
29	Capri Serenade	Musical - Jenny Jones	1944
30	Carnival in Spain	Song	1935
31	Carnival Song	Musical - Lisbon Story	1943
32	Come Out to Play	Revue - Come Out to Play	1940
33	Cottage of Dreams Come True	Song	c. 1924-8
34	Counting Sheep	Revue - The Shephard Show	1946
35	Cowslip Wine	Musical - Dear Miss Phoebe	1950
36	Crash, Bang I Want to Go Home	Revue - Black Velvet	1940
37	Croon to Me	Song	1934
38	Dearie	Operetta – The Curfew	1927
39	Diplomacy	Musical - Her Excellency	1949
40	Dirty Song	Revue - Big Top	1942
41	Disconcerto	Revue - The Shephard Show	1946
42	Don't Say Ha-ha to My Heart	Song	unknown
43	Down the Trail	Revue – High Time!	1946
44	Do You Remember My First Love Song	Film - Queen of Hearts	1936
45	Drifting	Song	c. 1924-8
46	Early in the Morning	Operetta - The Curfew	1927
47	Ending in Smoke	Revue - Fine Feathers	1945
48	'Erbert 'Enery 'Eppelthwaite (I want to be a Crooner)	Song	1935
49	Every Night Seven	Film – Suspected Person	1942
50	Farewell	Operetta – The Curfew	1927
51	Father in Heaven	Operetta – The Curfew	1927
52	Fine Feathers Make Fine Birds	Revue - Fine Feathers	1945
53	Follow My Dancing Feet	Musical - Full Swing	1942
54	Follow On Behind the Drum	Musical - Lisbon Story	1943
55	For the First Time I've Fallen in Love	Musical - Lisbon Story	1943

56	For the First Time in My Life I'm in Love	Film - Lassie from Lancashire	1938
57	Fount of Wisdom	Revue - Top of the World	1940
58	Full Swing	Musical - Full Swing	1942
59	Gangway	Revue – Gangway	1940
60	Gentlemen of Leisure	Revue - Best Bib and Tucker	1942
61	Getting Rid of It	Revue - Big Top	1942
62	Giddy Up	Film - Keep Smiling	1938
63	Glen Echo	Song	1948
64	Good Night Little Sweetheart	Film - Lassie from Lancashire	1938
65	Hail to Our Master	Operetta – The Curfew	1927
66	Happy Ending	Film - This Week of Grace	1933
67	Harbour Lights	Song	c. 1924-8
68	Heaven Will Be Heavenly	Revue – Gangway	1940
69	Here's to the Queen God Bless Her	Song	1940
70	Hey-Ho the Merry-O	Revue - Big Top	1942
71	High Hat Time	Revue - Fine Feathers	1945
72	Ho-dle-ay, Start the Day Right	Revue - Haw- Haw	1939
73	Home	Song	c. 1924-8
74	Hop, Skip and a Jig-Step	Musical - The Glorious Years	1952
75	How Beautiful You Are	Revue - Black Velvet	1940
76	If All the World Were Mine	Film - Sing As We Go	1934
77	I Can't Resist The Music	Musical - Dear Miss Phoebe	1950
78	I'd Like to Share My Life with You	Film - Candles at Nine	1944
79	I Fancy My Chances	Musical - Blue for a Boy	1950
80	If I Had a Girl Like You	Revue - Bell Bottom George	1944
81	If It's Wits that You Want	Operetta – The Curfew	1927
82	If This is Love	Musical - The Knight is Bold	1943
83	I Go on My Way Whistling	Musical - The Knight is Bold	1943
84	I Hate You (arranged from *The Curfew*)	Film- Look on the Bright Side	1932
85	I Leave My Heart in an English Garden	Musical - Dear Miss Phoebe	1950
86	I'm Peter the Pup amd I'm Twenty One To-day	Song	c.1927
87	I'm Telling Thee	Musical - The Knight is Bold	1943
88	In My Little Snapshot Album	Film - I See Ice	1938
89	In Pernambuco	Film - Shipyard Sally	1939
90	In Summer When Trees Be Green	Musical - The Knight is Bold	1943
91	I Shall Always Remember	Revue - The Shephard Show	1946
92	It All Comes Back to Me Now	Revue - The Shephard Show	1946

93	It Always Rains Before the Rainbow	Song	1941
94	It Happened One Sunday	Film - It Happened One Sunday	1944
95	It's in the Air	Film - It's in the Air	1938
96	I Want a Kiss From You	Operetta – The Curfew	1927
97	I Wonder	Musical – Her Excellency	1949
98	Joe the Jolly Mariner	Song	1935
99	Just a Catchy LittleTune	Film - Sing As We Go	1934
100	Kiss the Girls	Musical - The Knight is Bold	1943
101	Learn How to Live a Love Song	Film – Penny Paradise	1938
102	Lero, Lero, Lillibolero	Song	1950
103	Let's Have an Old-fashioned Christmas	Song	1937
104	Living a Dream	Musical - Dear Miss Phoebe	1950
105	Livvie's Had One of her Turns	Musical - Dear Miss Phoebe	1950
106	London is Saying Good Night	Song	1938
107	London Song	Revue - Big Top	1942
108	Lonely Serenade	Song	1940
109	Look Up and Laugh	Film - Look Up and Laugh	1935
110	Love Alone	Insertion in *Belle of New York*	1942
111	Love Finds a Way	Operetta – The Curfew	1927
112	Love Calling Me Home	Song	1950
113	Love is Everywhere	Film - Look Up and Laugh	1935
114	Love is Love Everywhere	Musical - Full Swing	1942
115	Love Never Grows Old	Song	1940
116	Love Stay in My Heart	Revue - Top of the World	1940
117	Lucky Me, Lucky You	Revue - Come Out to Play	1940
118	Lying Awake and Dreaming	Musical - Blue for a Boy	1950
119	Madame Louise	Musical – Lisbon Story	1943
120	Mamma Buy Me That	Musical - Full Swing	1942
121	March of the Redcoats	Musical - Dear Miss Phoebe	1950
122	March On	Operetta – The Curfew	1927
123	Mary Must Have Music	Revue - The Shephard Show	1946
124	Mary Rose	Film - This Week of Grace	1933
125	Maytime in Mayfair	Film - Maytime in Mayfair	1948
126	Merry Go Round	Musical - Jenny Jones	1944
127	Midnight Music	Musical - Lisbon Story	1943
128	Moon, Moon	Operetta – The Curfew	1927
129	Mother Nature	Musical - The Knight is Bold	1943
130	Music Makes Me Mad	Musical - Full Swing	1942
131	My Kind of Loving	Film - Women Aren't Angels	1944
132	My Kind of Music	Musical - Full Swing	1942
133	My Love for You	Film - The Show Goes On	1935

134	My Paradise	Revue – Gangway	1940
135	My Lucky Day	Film -This Week of Grace	1933
136	My Wish	Revue - Top of the World/	1940/
		Musical - Jenny Jones	1944
137	Never Say Goodbye	Musical -Lisbon Story	1943
138	Noughts and Crosses	Film - I See Ice	1938
139	Now and Forever	Film - Now and Forever	1955
140	Oh! Come All Ye People	Operetta – The Curfew	1927
141	One Song Shall Ever Remain	Film -Two Thousand Women	1944
142	Orchids in the Evening	Revue - Black Velvet	1940
143	Paris in My Heart	Film - Lisbon Story	1945
144	Paris Song	Revue - Big Top	1942
145	Passports for Two	Revue - The Shephard Show	1946
146	Pedro the Fisherman	Musical - Lisbon Story	1943
147	Peter the Penguin	Song	1948
148	Peter the Pup (See *Sing as We Go)*	Song	c. 1928
149	Praise to the Lord	Operetta – The Curfew	1927
150	Serenade for Sale	Musical - Lisbon Story	1943
151	She's Got That Look in Her Eyes	Song	1948
152	Shopping, Eating and the None O'clock News	Musical - Full Swing	1942
153	Sing a Happy-go-Lucky Song	Film - Three Sailors	1940
154	Sing as We Go (reworking of Peter the Pup c 1928)	Film- Sing as We go	1934
155	Smile When You Say Good-bye	Film - The Show Goes On	1935
156	Someday We'll Meet Again	Musical - Lisbon Story	1943
157	Song of April	Musical - The Glorious Years	1952
158	Song of the Sunrise	Musical - Lisbon Story	1943
159	Spring Will Sing a Song for You	Musical - Dear Miss Phoebe	1950
160	Stick Out Your Chin	Film – Penny Paradise	1938
161	Stop! It's Wonderful	Revue - Haw-Haw	1939
162	Success Cockalorum	Film - The Show Goes On	1935
163	Sunday Morning in England	Musical - Her Excellency	1949
164	Sweet Virginia	Revue - Fine Feathers	1940
165	Swing Your Way to Happiness	Film - Keep Smiling	1938
166	Swim Little Fish	Revue - Bell Bottom George	1944
167	Take the World Exactly As You Find It	Film – Happidrome	1942/3
168	Tell me Gypsy	Operetta – The Curfew	1927

169	The Angel (Fairy) on the Christmas Tree	Song	1936
170	The Glorious Years	Musical - The Glorious Years	1952
171	The Lady In Grey	Revue - Big Top	1942
172	The Little Swiss Yodelling song	Revue – Gangway	1940
173	The Love of a Lass	Musical - Dear Miss Phoebe	1950
174	The Night You sand 'O Sole Mio'	Song	1934
175	The Pretty Little Quaker Girl	Song	1938
176	There'll Be	Operetta – The Curfew	1927
177	There's a Trail That's Leading Back Home	Revue – High Time!	1946
178	The Shades of Night	Operetta – The Curfew	1927
179	The Show Goes On	Film - The Show Goes On	1935
180	The Song of England	Musical - The Glorious Years	1952
181	The Sweetest Girl in the World	Song	1938
182	The Sweetest Song in the World	Film – We're Going to be Rich	1938
183	The Trek Song	Film – We're Going to be Rich	1938
184	They Call Me a Dreamer	Revue - Come Out to Play	1940
185	The Years to Come	Song	1947
186	Things Might Have Been Different	Film - Look Up and Laugh	1935
187	Three Shades of Blue	Revue - Black Velvet	1940
188	Thro' Skies that Were Blue	Song	c. 1924-8
189	Tin Pan Alley's Plugger's Lament	Revue - Big Top	1942
190	Tradition	Musical - The Knight is Bold	1943
191	Tree Top Lullaby	Song	1934
192	Underneath the Moon in Old Shanghai	Song	c. 1924-8
193	Up the Hill to Windsor Castle	Musical - The Glorious Years	1952
194	Valley of Dreams	Film – It Happened One Sunday	1944
195	Very Odd Fish	Musical - Lisbon Story (tour)	1945
196	Wallflowers	Musical - Dear Miss Phoebe	1950
197	Wand'ring	Song	c. 1924-8
198	Well Done, Dean	Musical - The Knight is Bold	1943
199	Welcome the Bride	Musical - Jenny Jones	1944
200	We'll Going Smiling Along	Revue - Top of the World	1940
201	We're All Good Pals Together	Film - The Show Goes On	1935
202	We Shall Always Have To-day	Play – The Rest is Silence	1944
203	What Would You Do?	Revue - Top of the World	1940
204	When Cupid Calls	Film -This Week of Grace	1933

205	When I Hear the Music	Revue - Big Top	1942
206	When I was Young	Operetta – The Curfew	1927
207	When Will You Marry Me and Carry Me Home	Musical - Dear Miss Phoebe	1950
208	Where the Blue Begins	Revue - Top of the World/ Musical - Jenny Jones	1940/ 1944
209	Where the Rainbow Ends	Musical - Jenny Jones	1944
210	Whisper While You Waltz	Musical - Dear Miss Phoebe	1950
211	Whoopsy-Diddly-Dum-De-Dumm	Musical - The Knight is Bold	1943
212	Why Did I Have to Meet You	Film - Queen of Hearts	1936
213	Why Worry	Musical - Jenny Jones	1944
214	Wind Round My Heart	Revue - Big Top	1942
215	Wish Me Luck	Film - Shipyard Sally	1939
216	Yet Another Day	Musical - Jenny Jones	1944
217	You and the Moonlight	Musical - The Knight is Bold	1943
218	You Annoy Me So	Revue – Gangway	1940
219	You are My Love Song	Revue - Big Top	1942
220	You Can't Have Your Cake	Film – Penny Paradise	1938
221	Your Company's Requested at a Dream	Revue - Haw-Haw	1939
222	You've Got Him where You Want Him	Musical - Blue for a Boy	1950
223	You've Got to Smile When You Say Good-bye	Film - The Show Goes On	1935
224	You Only Want It 'Cos You Haven't It	Revue - Big Top	1942
225	Your Way is My Way	Film – No Limit	1936

Instrumental etc

No.	Title	Type	Year
1	Foxtrot	Piano	c. 1927-8
2	Legends	Piano solo	c. 1924-8
3	Le Rêve d'Amour	Violin solo	c. 1924-8
4	Mélodie	Organ solo	c. 1924-8
5	Nocturne	Violin solo	c. 1924-8
6	September in Capri	Piano solo	1940
7	Tesgar	Organ solo	c.1927
8	Foxtrot	Piano solo	c.1926

Orchestral

No.	Title	Type	Year
1	Ballet – Chanson de Paris	Revue - The Shephard Show	1946
2	My Capri Serenade	? Brass Band arrangement	1940
3	Overture, 2 introductions, an intermezzo and march	The Curfew	1927
3	Overture, ballet music and melos	Musical – Dear Miss Phoebe	1950
4	Overture, ballet music *St. Ceiriol*	Musical – Jenny Jones	1944
5	Overture, ballet music and melos	Musical – The Lisbon Story	1943

Query

Title	Comment	Year
There'll Always be an England	Usually credited to Ross Parker (possibly joint)	1940

Appendix 2

CHRONOLOGICAL LISTS
OF COMPOSITIONS

—⟡—

Abbreviations

    ABPC =Associated British Picture Corportion

    ATP= Associated Talking Pictures

Publishers:

    CA = Cameo Publishing Co., 23 Denmark St. WC2

    CH = Chappell Co. Ltd, 50 New Bond St. W1

    EM = Empire Publishing Co Ltd, 319 Oxford St. WC2

    FDH = Francis Day and Hunter & Co. Ltd, 138-140 Charing
        Cross Rd. WC2

    ID = Irwin Dash Music CO. Ltd, 10 Denmark St. London WC2

    KP = Keith Prowse & Co Ltd, 159 Bond St. W1

    LW = Lawrence Wright Music Co. Ltd, Denmark St. WC2

    PM=Peter Maurice, 21 Denmark St., WC2

    ST = Sterling Music Co. Ltd, 52 Maddox St.

    SU = Sun Music Publishing Co. Ltd, 23 Denmark St. WC2

    VI = The Victoria Music Publishing Co. Ltd, 51 Maddox
        St, WC2

Date of release/ first performance	Name	Type / source	Lyricist	Publisher where known	Musical Director and arranger
c. February 1922	For Princess Royal's Wedding	Song			
c.1924-8	Cottage of Dreams Come True	Song	Harry		
c.1924-8	Drifting	Song	Harry		
c.1924-8	Harbour Lights	Song	Harry		
c.1924-8	Home	Song	Judge Edward Abbott Parry		
c.1924-8	Thro' skies that were blue	Song	Harry		
c.1924-8	Mélodie	Violin solo			
c.1924-8	Legends	Piano solo			
c.1924-8	Le Rêve d'Amour	Violin solo			
c. 924-8	Nocturne	Violin solo			
c. 1926	Foxtrot	Piano solo			

1926-7	The Curfew	School Operetta	Harry's draft, but no music
	(Summary of score 25 vocal pieces, overture and 2 introduction at this stage planned –see Appendix 3)		
	Overture		
	Act I		
	1 - Opening Chorus *Oh! Come all ye people*		
	Dialogue I		
	2 - Scena *Hail to our Master*"		
	Dialogue II		
	3 - Duet and dance *Dearie*		
	Dialogue III		
	4 - Song and dance *When I was young*		
	Dialogue IV		
	5 - Finale (Scene I) *Tell me Gypsy*		
	6 – Baritone serenade, *Moon, Moon*		
	Dialogue V		
	7 - Soprano solo with chorus, prayer *Father in Heaven*		

Act II
8 - Chorus *Bring in the prisoner*
Dialogue VI
9 - Tenor solo *The shades of night*
Dialogue VII
10 - Mezzo solo *Its wits that you want*
Dialogue VIII
11 - Soprano solo *Love finds a way*
Dialogue IX
Dialogue X
12 - Duet *I Want a Kiss From You*
13 - Song *Early in the Morning*
14 - Intermezzo and chorus
15 - Finale with repeat of Prayer
Act III
16 - Introduction and duet *Farewell*
Dialogue XI
17 - solo reprise *Love finds a way*
18 - Soldiers March *March On*
19 - Priests Chorus *Praise to the Lord*
20 - Prayer *Father in Heaven*
21 - Soldiers March

	22 - Tenor solo reprise *The shades of night* Dialogue XII 23 - Soldiers March Dialogue XIII 24 Duet *There'll be* Dialogue XIV 25 Finale				
1927	Tesgar	March (Organ) for Tesgar Humphreys			
1928	Underneath the Moon in Old Shanghai	Song	Harry	EM	
1932 September	I Hate You	ATP Film - **Look on the Bright Side** Director Basil Dean	Harry	KP	Carol Gibbons
1933 14 September	A Melody at Dawn(Happy Ending Mary Rose My Lucky Day When Cupid Calls	Radio Picture Film – **This Week of Grace** Director Maurice Elvey	Gracie Fields Harry Gracie Fields Gracie Fields Harry	FDH	Thomas Percival Montague Mackey

1934 September	If All the World Were Mine	ATP Film - **Sing as We Go** Director Basil Dean	Harry	FDH	Ernest Irving
	Just a Catchy Little Tune				
	Sing as We Go				
	Croon to Me	Song	–		
	The Night You Sang 'O sole mio'	Song	–		
	Tree Top Lullaby	Song	Harry	KP	
	Blue Bird of Happiness	Song	Harry - words only		
1935 4 August	Anna from Anacapresi	ATP Film - **Look Up and Laugh** Director Basil Dean	Harry (with Horatio Nicholls)	LW	Ernest Irving
	Look Up and Laugh				
	Love is Everywhere				
28 October	Your Way is not My Way	ATP Film – **No Limit** Director Monty Banks	Harry		Ernest Irving
	Bring Back the Girl in the Old-fashioned Gown	Song			
	Carnival in Spain	Song			
	'Erbert 'Enery 'Epplethwaite	Song	Jeff Sullivan	FDH	
	Joe the Jolly Mariner	Song	John P. Long	KP	

Date	Song	Film / Director	Writer		Composer
1936 1 August	Binkie's Lullaby	ATP Film - **Keep Your Seats Please** Director Monty Banks	Arthur Wilson		Ernest Irving
5 October	Do You Remember My First Love Song Why Did I have to Meet You	ATP Film – **Queen of Hearts** Director Basil Dean	Harry Clifford Grey	SU	Ernest Irving
	The Angel (Fairy) on the Christmas Tree	Song	Roma Beaumont	SU	
1937 April	A Song in Your Heart My Love for You Smile when You Say Good-bye Success Cockalorum The Show Goes On We're All Good Pals Together	ATP Film - **The Show Goes On** Director Basil Dean	Eddie Pola Eddie Pola Harry Harry Will Haines and Jimmy Harper	LW CA	Ernest Irving
	Let's Have an Old-fashioned Christmas		Harry		

1938 10 February	In My Little Snapshot Album Noughts and Crosses	ATP Film – **I See Ice** Director Anthony Kimmins	Will Haines and Jimmy Harper Roma Campbell-Hunter	LW	Ernest Irving
3 July (USA)	The Sweetest Song in the World The Trek Song	20th Century Fox Film – **We are Going to be Rich** Director Monty Banks	Harry Harry	FDH CH	Bretton Byrd
August	For the First Time in My Life I'm in Love Good Night Little Sweetheart	British National Production Film – **Lassie From Lancashire** Director John Paddy Carstairs	Harry Harry	KP	Ronnie Munro
24 September	Learn How to Live a Love Song Stick Out Your Chin You Can't Have Your Cake and Eat It	ATP Film – **Penny Paradise** Director Carol Reed	Harry Harry Harry	KP	Ernest Irving and Gideon Fagan

November	It's in the Air	ATP Film – **It's in the Air** Director Anthony Kimmins	Harry	KP	Ernest Irving
December	Giddy Up Swing Your Way to Happiness	20th Century Fox Film – **Keep Smiling** Director Monty Banks	Harry Harry	FDH	Bretton Byrd
	London is Saying Goodnight	Song	Harry (with Horatio Nicholls and Roma Campbell-Hunter)	LW	
	Mother, Mother, Mother, Mother	Song	Harper and Haines	LW	
	The Sweetest Girl in the World	Song			
	The Sweetest Sweetheart of All	Song	Joe Messini	ID	

1939 20 October	In Pernambuco Wish' Me Luck	20th Century Fox Film –**Shipyard Sally** Director **Monty Banks**	Harry Phil Park	CH	Louis Levy
14 November	Bubble, Bubble Crash! Bang! I Want to Go Home How Beautiful You are Orchids in the Evening Three Shades of Blue	George Black's Revue –**Black Velvet** Producer **Robert Nesbitt**	Roma Campbell-Hunter Ralph Butler Phil Park Roma Campbell-Hunter Harry	CH	Debroy Somers
22 December	As 'Round and 'Round We Go Ho-dle-ay Start the Day Right Stop! It's Wonderful Your Company's Requested	George Black's Revue – **Haw Haw**	Phil Park	ST	
	Love Never Grows Old	Song	Harry	CH	
	Little Swiss Yodelling Song The	Song	Harry	CH	

	Pretty Little Quaker Girl	Song	Roma Campbell-Hunter	CH	
1940 19 March	Come Out to Play Lucky Me, Lucky You Things are Going to be Different	George Black's Revue - **Come Out to Play**		ST	
23 March	Heaven Will be Heavenly	Gainsborough Film - **Band Waggon** Director Marcel Varnel	Barbara Gordon and Basil Thomas	CH	Louis Levy
7 August (closed after 4 days)	Alone With You Fount of Wisdom Love Stay in My Heart My Kind of Music My Wish We'll Go Smiling Along What Would You Do? Where the Blue Begins Why Worry Yet Another Day	George Black's Revue – **Top of the World**	Phil Park	CH	

					Ernest Irving
14 December	Sing a Happy-Go-Lucky Song	Ealing Studios Film – **Sailors Three** Director Walter Forde	Phil Park		Ernest Irving
	Here's To Her Majesty God Bless Her	Song	Phil Park	CH	
	Lonely Serenade	Song - for Lew Stone	Roma Campbell-Hunter	CH	
	My Capri Serenade	Song	Harry	CH	
	September in Capri – An Italian Picture	Piano			
1941 9 March	So Deep in the Night (Vocal arrangement of Chopin ballade for Zeigler and Booth)	George Black Revue - **Gangway**			
	Gangway My Paradise You Annoy Me So		Barbara Gordon and Basil Thomas		
	It Always Rains Before the Rainbow	Song	Gordon Orbell and Harry	CH	
1942 P 18 February L 16 April	Be Refined (cut) Follow My Dancing Feet Full Swing Love is Love Everywhere Mamma Buy Me That	George Black Musical - **Full Swing**	Barbara Gordon and Basil Thomas	CH	

Date	Show	Song		CH
		Music Makes Me Mad		
		Shopping, Eating and the Nine O'Clock News		
		You Only Want It 'cos You Haven't Got It		
8 May	Charles B Cochrane's Revue - **Big Top**	Getting Rid of It with Geoffrey Wright (music) Hey-Ho the Merry-O	Herbert Farjeon	CH
			Barbara	
		The Lady in Grey - Wind 'Round My Heart Tin Pan Alley Plugger's Lament	Gordon and Basil Thomas	
			Barbara	
		When I Hear Music	Gordon and Basil Thomas	
			Barbara	
		You are My Love Song	Gordon and Basil Thomas	
			Barbara	
		You Only Want It Because You Haven't Got It	Gordon and Basil Thomas	
			Barbara	
			Gordon and Basil Thomas	
			Barbara	
			Gordon and Basil Thomas	

June	Every Night at Seven	ABP Film- **Suspected Person** Director Lawrence Huntington	Barbara Gordon and Basil Thomas	CH	Charles Williams
L 16 September	Love Alone	Insertion song – revival of musical **Belle of New York**	Adrian Foley	CH	
7 November	Best Bib and Tucker Gentlemen of Leisure	George Black's Revue - **Best Bib and Tucker**	Barbara Gordon and Basil Thomas		Debroy Somers
1943 18 January	All the World Sings a Lullaby	Columbia British Film –**We'll Meet Again** Director Philip Brandon	Barbara Gordon and Basil Thomas	CH	Harry Bidgood

18 January	My Kind of Loving	ABPC Film – **Women Aren't Angels** Director Lawrence Huntington	Harold Purcell		Charles Williams
P 31 May	Overture Carnival Song Follow on Behind the Drum For the First Time I've Fallen in Love Madame Louise Midnight Music Never Say Goodbye Pedro the Fisherman Serenade for Sale Someday we'll Meet Again Song of the Sunrise Ballet Music Many Melos	George Black's Musical – **The Lisbon Story**	Harold Purcell	CH	
7 June	Take the World Exactly As You Find It You are My Love Song	Aldwych Film – **Happidrome** Director Philip Brandon	Phil Park	CH	Bretton Byrd

Date	Songs	Production			
1 July	If This is Love I Go on My Way Whistling I'm Telling Thee Kiss the Girls Mother Nature Tradition Well Done, Dean Whoopsy-Diddly-Dum-de Dumm You and the Moonlight	George Black Musical –**The Knight was Bold** Basil Thomas	Barbara Gordon		Phil Green
1944 18 January	I'd Like to Share My Love with You	British National Film – **Candles at Nine** Director John Harlow	Harold Purcell	VI	Charles Williams
7 February	Bell Bottom George If I Had A Girl Like You Swim Little Fish	Columbia British Film – **Bell Bottom George** Director Marcel Varnel	Phil Park		Harry Bidgood
20 April	We Shall Have To-day	Play by Harold Purcell – **The Rest of Silence**	Harold Purcell	CH	

28 July	All Ashore, Valley of Dreams	ABPC Film - **It Happened One Sunday** Director Karel Lumac	Harry Harry	CH	Charles Williams
P 12 September L 2 October	After All Annabella My Wish* Where the Blue Begins* Where the Rainbow Ends Why Worry* Yet Another Day* Ballet Music	George Black's Musical - **Jenny Jones**	Harold Purcell	CH*	
1945 October	Ending in Smoke Fine Feathers Make Fine Birds High Hat Time Sweet Virginia	Robert Nesbitt Revue – **Fine Feathers**	Phil Park Phil Park Phil Park Phil Park	CH	George Melachrino
	April in the Spring of Love Very Odd Fish	George Black's Musical- **The Lisbon Story** (provincial tour)	Harold Purcell	CH	Hans May

Date	Title	Work	Lyricist	Code	
1946 2 February	Paris in My Heart	Film - **The Lisbon Story** Director Paul L Stein	Harold Purcell	CH	
20 April	Down the Trail	Val Parnell revue **High Time!**			
26 September	A Song and Story / Bubbling Over / Chanson de Paris – ballet / Counting Sheep / Disconcerto / I Shall Always Remember / It All Comes Back to Me Now / Mary Must Have Music / Passports for Two	Firth Shephard's Revue -**The Shephard Show**	Harold Purcell	ST	
1947	The Years to Come	Song	Douglas Furber	CH	
1948	Angela Mia	Song	Harold Purcell		
	Annette	Song			
	Glen Echo	Song		CH	
	Peter the Penguin	Song	Harold Purcell	CH	

				CH	
1949 19 April	Diplomacy I Wonder Sunday Morning in England	Bernard Delfont Musical – **Her Excellency**	Harold Purcell		
24 May	Maytime in Mayfair	British Lion Film Corporation Film – **Maytime in Mayfair** Director Herbert Wilcox	Harold Purcell		Robert Farnon
1950 P 31 July L 13 October	Overture A Certain Individual All's well Tonight Cowslip Wine I Can't Resist the Music I Leave My Heart in an English Garden Living A Dream Livvie's Had One of Her Turns March of the Redcoats Spring Will Sing a Song for You The Love of a Lass Wallflowers When Will You Marry Me and Carry Me Home Whisper While You Waltz Ballet Music and Melos	Musical – **Dear Miss Phoebe** Producer Charles Hickman	Christopher Hassall	SU	Philip Martel

P 14 August L 13 October	A Little Bit on Account At Last It Happened A Year Ago To-day Blue for a Boy I Fancy My Chance Lying Awake and Dreaming You've Got Him Where You Want Hi	Emile Littler's Musical –**Blue for a Boy or what Shall we do with the Body**	Harold Purcell	SU
1951 Summer	Lero Lero, Lillibulero	Song of the Festival Fires (Festival of Britain)	Harold Purcell	SU
	Love Calling Me Home	Song	Barbara Gordon	SU
1952 P November 1953 L 28 February	Bird Cage Walk A Hop, Skip and a Jigstep Song of April The Glorious Years The Song of England Up the Hill to Windsor Castle (only song used in film version **Lilacs in Spring**	Tom Arnold Musical – **Glorious Years**	Harold Purcell	SU

1955	In preparation			
		Musical - **Marry Me Margaret**	Harold Purvcell	
		Musical – Caroline	Harold Purcell	
		Musical – an Ivor Novello play	Christopher Hassall	
1956 21 February	Now and Forever	Film - **Now and Forever**	Christopher Hassall	PM

Appendix 3

THE DRAFT TEXT OF 'THE CURFEW'

"The Curfew"

(transcribed from Harry's exercise book.)[132]

An operetta in Three Acts

Partly based on the narrative poem entitled "The Curfew shall not toll (sic) tonight"

written and composed by Harry Parr-Davies aged 13 years

---

[132] Repeats are indicated but not written out again. The denouément is as given but historical anomalies are noted in footnotes. This MSS would seem to be an early draft rather than a performing edition.

=======

<u>Dramatis Personae</u>

Marie Blanche...a village maiden

Jack Courtnay...her lover

Lord Gerard de Maur..a callous lord

Oliver Cromwell ....

Madame Grenfell ....the Village Gossip

An old Bellringer...

A Captain of the Guard ....

Judge Barton ....a Judge

Janet, Elizabeth, and Charles

~~A witness~~..

1ˢᵗ Juryman..

2ⁿᵈ Juryman...

~~Father Joseph Vaughn~~ .... a priest

A Gypsy

~~An accomplice of Charles I~~

Squire Courtnay...father of Jack

Papa Oldham .... an old villager

Nan Oldham... his daughter

Chorus and Villagers, soldiers, Priests, and Jury

Period

The early part of the Seventeenth Century.

Synopsis

When the story opens, it is "Harvest Time" and the villagers are enjoying themselves. Suddenly upon the scene comes a callous French Lord by the name of Gerald de Maur.He is attracted by the looks of Marie Blanche, a village maiden who is in love with the Squire's son, Jack Courtnay. Jack threatens Gerald de Maur with his life if he makes love to Marie again.

Gerald de Maur consults a gypsy, as o whom he loves, and the answer is, that he loves Marie Blanche, but, it is dangerous for him to make love to her.

That night he makes love to her and is shot. Jack is accused of murdering him, and is put into prison, until he can be tried.

The next day he is tried for his life, and is found guilty. He is sentenced to death at the ringing of the Curfew the following night.

Marie begs the old bell ringer, who is deaf, not to ring the bell that night; but he refuses.

It is nearing the time for the execution when Marie thinks of a plan. Her plan is climb the belfry and stop the bell as it moves.

She carries out her plan, and seeing Cromwell coming over the hills, she falls at his feet and begs for Jack's life. He grants her request, and he also brings with him, proof of Jack's innocence.

Mysteries cleared, all ends in song and dance.

Scenery

Act I (scene I)   The Village Green (Scene II) Same Night

Act II   The Court Room

Act III	Interior of Prison and Church
Act I	Scene I
No. I	Opening Chorus 'Oh! Come all ye people'

Chorus:-

"Oh! Come all ye people, and join with us in song
For, we must depart to, the fields ere long
And then with a rake, and then with a hoe,
We'll start with our work again, as of yore"

Papa Oldham:-

I am a poor papa old, you'd tell me by my name
Tho' I am four score five years, I'm not so much as lame,
For all my troubles, burst like bubbles
So should yours too.
Oh! Dance about forget your troubles, as I always do.

Refrain:-

So Follow this way, follow that way but wherever you go
Mind to call at wheat fields, with a rake and a hoe.
Come back this way, come back that way but wherever you go
Mind to pay a friendly call, in at the "Head of the Boar".

(Chorus in unison):-

Repeat refrain

Papa Oldham:-

I had a loved one, but she's gone some twenty years ago
In joining her, I shan't be long, to love her all the more.
And she'll come to meet me, and to greet me
In the heavens above
Oh! Then how happy will I be, up there where all is love.

Refrain:-

Repeat refrain

(Chorus in unison):-

Repeat refrain and

Chorus:-	repeat 1ˢᵗ 4 lines
Madame Grenfell:-	Stay for a moment, I've some news to tell,' 'Tis very important, and will not bode us well.
Chorus:-	Put down your rake, and put down your hoe.

And stay for a moment before we go

Then on to the wheat fields, with song and then a dance.

So come with your chatter, while you've a chance.

Dialogue I

Madame G:-	Now perhaps, I'll tell you the news."
Chorus:- (excitedly)	"Hurrah hurrah, the news, the news."
Mdme G:-	"Do not get excited, and I do wish you wouldn't push so."
Papa Oldham:-	"Aye, silence there, silence."
Mdme G:-	"Well, I will continue. As you know, my master, the Squire went up to London last week, and, he has not returned. He has sent e this letter, explaining why he has not returned. I will read it to you." (reads)

Dear Jane,

I have been here a good while now, and, I hope to return to-day. When I got in London, I was greatly surprised to find the streets deserted; and driving on I came to a crowd of people, standing outside Westminster Hall. I enquired into the matter, and found out that Our Royal sovereign, King Charles I was on trial for High Treason.

I expect this will interest you greatly, and give you a topic for a few days. I am bringing home with me a new friend, by the name of, Lord Gerald de Maur. I trust you will give him a good welcome.

Your sincere master, and friend,

Silas Courtnay.

There, what do you think of that?"

Nan O:-	"Positively disgraceful."
Papa O:-	"Most shocking"
Nan O:-	"Terribly alarming."
Papa O:-	"Exactly so"
Nan O:-	"'Tis almost incredible, isn't it? All I hope is,that it will put an end, to this dreadful Civil War."
Madame G:-	"So do I, but here comes our master and his new friend."
Chorus:-	"Hurrah hurrah hail to our master, and, his friend." (enter Squire Courtnay and Lord Gerald de Maur with followers.)
No. 2	Scena "Hail to our Master"
Chorus:-	Hail to our Master, hail to his friend; Hail to their escorts, whom, Liberty defend. Welcome are they in, our village small; On this jolly harvest day, come and join us all.
Squire Courtnay:-	Yonder stands a noble peer, He is worthy of your cheer, In your praises never fail, Never fail; Hail him as you'd hail a king, Aye and make the welkin ring,

To his praises gladly sing, Aye gladly sing.

Chorus:-   repeat above

Gerald de Maur:-   Just across the silv'ry sea,
In sunny France;
There how happy will I be

In sunny France;

For all my servants love me well,
Their gratitude I earn;
And if you too would love me true,
Why! French then you must learn.

Refrain:-   Bon jour, monsieur,
Pardonnez moi, mam'selle,
Bon jour means good morning,
You understand quite well;
Pardonnez moi means pardon me,
For any slight mistake,
And in that land of courtesy,
Mistakes you must not make.

(Chorus in unison):-   Repeat above

French soldiers:-   Allons enfants de la Patrie
Le jour de gloire est arrive:
Contre nous de la tyrannie,
L'étendard sanglant est levé
Entendez vous dans les compagnes
Mugir ces forces soldats.
Ils viennent jusque dans vos bras
Égorger vos fils vos compagnes.
Aux armes citoyens!
Formez des bataillons
Marchons, Marchons
Qu'un sang impur

A breuvé nos sillons.[133]

Chorus:-	Oh! Come and join us in the fun,
	Our cups of joy have overrun,
	Upon this jolly Harvest Day,
	Oh! Let your troubles fly away;;
	Let a lassie chose her lad,
	And merrily we'll say
	'Tis God alone has made us glad
	Upon this Harvest Day.

All:-   Repeat last 4 lines

Dialogue II

Gerald de Maur:-   "I thank you, my friends for the kind reception you have given me."

Squire Courtnay: "Do not mention your Lordship, I am sure it is a pleasure to the villagers, is it not?"

Chorus:-   "Aye, aye, that it is."
G de Maur:- (aside)
"I am positively charmed by the looks of this beautiful maiden to the right of me ~~can be.~~ I wonder who she -can be. However I will ~~con~~ enquire. (aloud) My dear Courtnay, who is this charming maiden here (pointing to Marie)

Squire Courtnay:-   "That is Marie Blanche, the unrivalled belle of the village. Come forward, Marie"   (Marie comes forward)

G de M:-   "Hello, little girl. I was so charmed by your looks, that I had to enquire after you."

Marie:-   "Your Lordship flatters me."

---

[133]   Claude Joseph Roguet de Lisle's anthem dates from 1792!

G de M:-	"Not at all, I simply give you your due. But, I say, do you believe in love at first sight? (Chorus laugh)
Mdme G:-(aside)	"How very, romantic he is."
Marie:-	"Your Lordship perplexes me, but, I think I can answer that question."
G de M:-	"Well, what is your answer?"
Marie:-	"No, and nothing else. Your Lordship must understand that I have a lover, whom I love better than anything in the world."
G de M:-	"Pshaw, girl. 'Tis but a feeble excuse." (Jack comes foward) "Who is this impertinent knave?."
Squire Courtnay:-	"Your Lordship, he is my son."
Gerald de Maur:-	"Your son? Mon Dieu, he is er- rather of a bloodthirsty nature, is he not?
Squire Courtnay:-	"Not as a rule, your Lordship. But if your lordship wishes it, I will punish him according to your desires"
G. de Maur:-	"No, no it doesn't matter now, but, I hope it will not occur again. Now then, what about retiring, for I am tired after a long journey. Shall we go?"
Squire C:-	"Certainly, your Lordship certainly."
G. de Maur:-	"Let us depart then au revoir."
Chorus:-	"Au river your Lordship, au river"

(Exit Lord Gerald de Maur, Squire Courtnay and followers.)

Papa O:	"Now then on to the wheatfields"

Chorus:-	"Hurrah, hurrah on to the wheatfields" (exit all except Marie and Jack)
Marie:-	"Dearie"
Jack:-	"Dearie"
(both):-	"I love you, and you love me"

No. 3	Duet and Dance (Marie and Jack)	"Dearie"

Jack:-	When a maiden woos a man, All she has to do: Is to stretch out her left hand, And say how I love you.
Marie:-	But that maiden may be shy,
Jack:-	Possibly like me:
Marie:-	What are they then both to do,
Jack:-	Just the same as we.
Refrain:-	
(Jack)	Dearie
(Marie)	Dearie
(Both)	I love you and you love me
(Jack)	Dearie
(Marie)	Dearie
(Both)	How happy we two could be Faithful to one another. We'd live and die;

Just dreaming and dreaming, not plotting and schemeing
Just you and I. Dance

Dialogue III

(exit Marie and Jack dancing)(Chorus gradually enter on tip toes peeping after Marie and Jack)

Mdme G:-	"Did you see them?"
Papa O:-	"What! trust me"
Madame G:-	"Oh! Of course, trust you. You know everything you do. "But to return to the subject. It takes me back to my younger days when I was woo'd, by a Lord of High Degree –very much like the one, who is at present staying here."
Chorus:-	"Tell us of your romance Madame.
Madame G:-	"Ah! No, I cannot. My heart is too full to relate my past.

(Chorus nudge each other as if in sympathy.)

Papa O:-	"Oh! Do let us be brighter. Remember it is Harvest Day."
Nan O:-	"Yes. Well what about making a start Papa."
Papa O:-	"By all means, but, how shall I begin"
Madame G:-	"By giving us a song.
Papa O:-	"Ah a good idea. Shall I sing to you of when I was yung. No. 4 Song and Dance (Papa Oldham) "When I was Young"

191

Papa O:-   Listen while I tell you of my younger days,
The days when no-one had a hold on me;
I know 'tis hard to think,
That I've got no missing link,
But it's quite as true as true can be.
Now I'm old and shaken, but that does not alter,
What I now am going to say to you,
So sit and listen there,
For it isn't very fair,
For me to be so bright and you so blue.
Until I met the one.
And that's my wife that's dead and buried and is gone,
If she were here to-day I'd never sing this song,
When I was young I was so handsome and so gay,
Oh! Yes, when I was young.

Chorus:- (in unison)   When he was young, he was so handsome and so gay,
Oh! Yes when he was young.
He had a different sweetheart nearly ev'ry day,
Until he met the one.
And that's his wife that's dead and buried and is gone,
If she were here to-day he'd never sing this song,
When he was young he was so handsome and so gay,
Oh! Yes, when he was young.

Dialogue IV

Chorus:-   "Bravo Papa, bravo."

Mdme G:-   "Who would have thought, that an old man of your age, could dance and sing as you have done. You really have charmed me, and deserve good praise."

Papa O:-	"Do not mention it Madame. I endeavoured to brighten you up. I hope I have succeeded."
Mdme G:-	You have, and very well too. But, stay, who is this approaching? I do declare it is that French Lord, Gerald de Maur again."
Papa O:-	"But the Squire is not with him."
Mdme G:-	"No, a gypsy has taken his place. Now I wonder what he wants with a gypsy?"
Nan O:-	"Undoubtedly, he wants his fortune told"
Mdme G:-	"Of course. A wonder I did not think of that before. . Let us hide, and listen to what goes on between them."
Papa O:-	"No need to hide, for here they are.
Chorus:-	"Hurrah, hurrah, long live his Lordship."

(enter G de M with a Gypsy, behind them come G de M's followers.

No.5	Finale (Scene I) "Tell me Gypsy"
G de M:-	Tell me Gypsy, tell me true; Whom I love the best tell me whom. Your life will forfeit be, If you cannot satisfy me.
Chorus:-	Tell him Gypsy, tell me true; Whom he loves the best tell him true. Your life your forfeiting, If you cannot satisfy him.
Gypsy:-	Tarry, tarry, Where is my fee?
G de M:-	Hurry, hurry, It shall double be Tell him Gypsy, tell me true;

Whom he loves the best tell him true.
Your life your forfeiting,
If you cannot satisfy him.

Gypsy:-

"You say you love a maiden,
You know not whom she is,
Why should you ask a gypsy?
(Her (His) knowledge thus to quiz.
'Tis no use asking anyone,
Your heart should direct you;
And if that does not Well,
What you going to do ?

G de M:-

"Today I met a maiden,
With whom I fell in love;
She seem'd just like an angel,
Straight from the heaven above.

Gypsy:-

"Ah! That then is the maiden,
Whom you love with all your heart;
And having fallen in love with her
You'll find it hard to part.
Make love to this maiden,
This fair pretty maiden,
Reward shall be greater than kingdom or part;
Be cautious in wooing,
For death is pursuing,
You as your making your way to her heart. (Twice)
Chorus:-(in unison) Make love to this maiden etc

Curtain end of Scene I

Scene II

No 6 Serenade (G de Maur and Marie)

G de M:-

Moon, moon, moon,
Bright in radiant splendour,
Look down from your lofty seat,

And bless her and defend her,
The nightingale its song is ended,
Night has cast her deadly pall
Moon, moon, moon,
Shine down and bless us all.

Marie (from window of house on right hand side where a candle is
        burning):-
    Sail, my boat of dreams
    Answer my prayer;
    Down the silv'ry streams,
    To my love.
    (G de M and Marie)   Sail, my boat of dreams
    etc
    Shine you bright moonbeams,
    Shine your brightest gleams
    From above.
    Father in heaven,
    Answer my prayer;
    Sail my boat of dreams.

(As the last bar is played, a shot is heard and G de M falls to the ground.
Marie screams and rushes down from her room and bends over G de M.

Dialogue V (enter chorus carrying candles)

Mdme G:-   "What is the meaning of all this commotion at
                         this time of --------? (screams and drops candle
                         on seeing G de M's body) How is this? What has
                         happened.?"

Marie;-   "I- I- I don't know."

Mdme G:-   "Come girl be reasonable, and tell us what has
                         happened.?"

Marie;-   "I- I- I will tell you all I know, that is to say not
                         much."

Papa O:-   "Well."

Marie:-	"It was like this. I was retiring for the night, when, I heard a voice singing beneath my window. I looked out and manafed to discern a figure whom I recognised as Gerald de Maur I rushed from the room, in time to see a figure rush off; laughing to himself as he went. A second after that, Gerald de Maur gave his last breath, and died.
Nan O:-	"How strange --------.
Mdme G:-	"It is not strange at all. Are you all blind?: Cannot you see? What did Jack Courtnay say this morning? What did that Gypsy prophesy? The real murderer is of course Jack Courtnay, and she (pointing to Marie) naturally is trying to shield him"
Nan O:-	"Oh! Madame how can you say so. I am quite sure that is not the case.
Mdme G;-	"Be silent. No one asked you to speak. Go back to your bed. You are only a nuisance and nothing else. Oh! Yes go on you. It would not be you, unless you went exactly opposite to (what) anyone said.
Papa O:-	"I would rather think you who does all that business."

"But as I was saying it is Jack Courtnay is the murderer. Do you all agree?

Chorus :-	"Aye, aye, we agree, we agree."
Mdme G:-	"Then all we have to do is to have him arrested and tried, and another thing, it is dangerous to have such a criminal at large. One does not know who is to be his next victim
Marie:-	"Madame how dare you say such things about my lover, who is as innocent as you yourself."

No 7   Prayer (Marie)

(Marie kneels down in the middle of the stage with her hands crossed)
                          Father in heaven,
                          Heed to my humble prayer;
                          Spare him oh! spare him,
                          He is to me so dear.
                          Father in heaven,
                          Heed to my humble prayer;
                          Keep him oh! keep him,
                          Keep him from danger there.
                          (soft voices are heard)   repeat above 4 lines

Curtain end of Act I

Act II

Introductory Chorus   "Bring in the prisoner"

Chorus:-   Bring in the prisoner,
                       Bring in the prisoner, Bring in the prisoner that's
                       guilty of crime,
                       Bring in the prisoner, Bring in the prisoner,
                       Bring in the prisoner he's wasting our time,
                       Bring in the prisoner, Bring in the prisoner,
                       Bring in the prisoner, the jury and judge
                       Bring in the prisoner, Bring in the prisoner,
                       Bring in the prisoner, we bear him no grudge

Jury:-   "To-day we bring a prisoner,
                       Accused of murdering,
                       A rival whom he'd threatened,
                       A very wicked thing.
                       We are not very sure of course,
                       To prison he was sent;
                       Some of us think he's guilty,
                       And other innocent.

Marie:-   I swear he is,

Dame G.:-	I swear he's not
Both:-	I don't care what you say.
Marie:-	I swear he is,
Dame G.:-	I swear he's not
Both:-	Oh ! hush all your arguing
Judge B:-	I won't have this in my court, For all your words they come to naught. I don't care what you say. You'll say not another thing. This question is, So difficult,
Chorus:-	This question is, So difficult, You don't know when your (you're) right or wrong, This question is, So difficult, Oh! Come join us all in song.
All	
{Marie:-	I swear he is,
{Judge B.:-	I will not have
{Chorus:-	This question is,
{Marie:-	I swear he is,
{Dame G.:-	I swear he's not
{Chorus:-	So difficult.
Chorus:-	Bring in the prisoner, Bring in the prisoner, Bring in the prisoner, the jury and judge,

Bring in the prisoner, Bring in the prisoner
Bring in the prisoner we bear him no grudge,
(twice)

Dialogue VI

Janet:-

"I wonder where the prisoner is?"

Eliz:-

"Sh- do not say anything, but they think he has escaped"

Mdme G:-

"Escaped? Did I hear you hear you say escaped?"

Eliz:-

"Yes, you did"

Mdme G:-

"Impossible. I visited the prisoner this morning, and then he was guarded by four soldiers besides the Captain of the Guard.

Eliz:-

"Well; however, the rumour has it about that he has escaped."

Mdme G:-

"Fortunately, it is not true."

Charles:-

"Why fortunately Madame

Mdme G:-

"I have my own reasons, and I do not care to discuss them now."

Janet:-

"We are greatly surprised at you Madame. You have been employed by the Squire this twenty three years now, and you have said that he has been a good master to you, but yet you go against him in this matter, when he is most in need of a friend.

Madame G:-

"Hold you willing tongue child, the Judge is about to speak."

Judge Barton:-

"Silence in court. Bring in the prisoner.

(enter Jack in a ruffled condition) Prisoner, what is your name?"

Jack:-   "Jack Courtnay, your worship."

Judge B:-   "Where do you reside?."

Jack:-   "At the Manor House Redlam.[134]".

Judge B:-   "Am I to understand that you are arrested on account of having murdered a man.".

Jack:-   "You are, your worship, tho' the charge be false."

Judge B:-   "Whether the charge be false or no will e left to be seen. Silence in court. Bring in the prisoner.

Jack:-   "Your worship. I crave a boon."

Judge B:-   "Providing it is a small one, it is granted."

Jack:-   "I crave to sing a song my mother taught me when I was young."

Judge B:-   "Your boon is granted."

No. 9   Ballad (Jack)   "The shades of night"

Jack   The shades of night are falling,
                         The Curfew bell doth toll;
                         Its dark and solemn warning,
                         Its warning aye to all.
                         Aye thro' the evening pealing,
                         Those chimes so dear to all
                         Across the night air stealing
                         In answer to my call.
                         The night comes long and dreary,
                         With many anxious cares;
                         That make a heart so weary,

---

[134]   There is a Redlam as a district of Blackburn; here the name is surely fictional.

But day its wounds repairs.
How soon the night is over,
And dawn doth break again;
And in the sun the clover,
Doth raise its head again.
Repeat 8 lines of above The shades of night are falling,

Dialogue VII

Judge B:-	"That old song has seen many years, but nevertheless it (is) none the worse for its agedness"
Jack:-	"No, your worship, it is as sweet to me as when I first learnt it."
Judge B:-	"I must not let my mind wander, or else we will never complete our business. Now, then, prisoner, what were you doing on the night of the murder?"
Jack:-	"I was at home, improving my knowledge."
Judge B:-	"What time was it when you were arrested?" .
Jack:-	"Twenty minutes past two o'clock in the morning."
Judge B:-	"Who discovered the crime?" .
Jack:-	"Madame Grenfell, your worship"
Judge B:-	"Let her be brought forward" .
Mdme G:-	"I will not brought forward at all. I will come forward of my own (will)"

(She comes forward and goes in witness stand)

Judge B:-	"Now then witness" .
Mme G:-	"Madame, if you please"

Judge B:-
"Well then, Madame. How did you discover the crime>".

Madame G (indifferently):-
"Oh! Just a matter of course, that is all. Only another example of my wits. It has been said that I have the eyes of an eagle, meaning of course that nothing escapes them. Let me tell you my man it's what you want and it's wits I've got. I see that I keep them about me. my man"

No. 10
Song (Madame Grenfell)   "It is wits that you want"
It is wits you want and its wits I've got;
And I see that I keep them about me,
It is wits you want and its wits I've got;
Not a soul in the village will doubt me.
For Christmas time comes once a year,
And when it comes it brings good cheer;
It is wits you want and its wits I've got;
And I see that I keep them about me,
When Christmas is drawing nigh,
And around the fire we sit
I am the spark that sets the light;
With my little bit of wit.

Chorus:-
It is wits you want and its wits I've got;
And I see that I keep them about me,
When Christmas is drawing nigh,
And around the fire we sit
am the spark that sets the light;
With my little bit of wit.

Dialogue VIII

Judge B:-
"You said you were the first to discover the crime. Did you?"

Mdme G:-   "Yes, I did."

Judge B:-   "How was it the that this opportunity for showing your wonderful wits came about?"

Mdme G:-   "I will relate the whole story as I know it for the beginning to end (coughs and prepared herself as if for an ordeal) Yesterday, as you know, was Harvest Day, the most important day on the year. Well, however it happened that the Squire went to London last week, where he met a friend, whom he brought home with him.

Judge B:-   And, what pray, has that to do with his assassination?"

Mdme G:-   "Have patience man, have patience. I am coming to the point. As I said, this friend was no other than the deceased, Lord Gerald de Maur.

Chorus:-   "Bravo, Madame, bravo

Janet:-   "Pshaw, fancy saying bravo to that old duck, who at her best can only quack."

Mdme G:-   "Since you are so clever perhaps you do better?"

Judge B:-   "Silence in court. We must proceed with the trial, for delays are dangerous. Now then, Madame, perhaps you can inform us further upon this matter."

Mdme G:- (sarcastically)

"Oh! Certainly, certainly anything to oblige. Have patience, man have patience. I am coming to the point. As I said, this friend was no other than the deceased.Lord Gerald de Maur. Naturally on going to the Squire's house, they had to pass through the Village, where we were all assembled. He was attracted by the beauty of Marie Blanche, the Belle of our village, and he asked if she believed in love at first sight. No sooner had he said that than Jack Courtnay and threatened him with his life, of he spoke to her again. That afternoon, however he consulted a Gypsy as to whom he loved and his answer was he loved Marie Blanche, but it was too dangerous for Him to make love to her. That night despite these warnings he made love to her and was shot. Now what more evidence do you want than that?"

Judge B:-

"None, I assure you, but, as there is another witness, we must give her a hearing, especially as she is the cause of the murder. Let her be brought forward. (Madame G comes out of the witness box and Marie takes her place.) Witness, am I to understand that you are the betrothed of the prisoner?

Marie:-

"You are, your worship."

Judge B:-

"Tell us then how the crime was com(m)itted?"

Marie:-

"It was like this. I was retiring for the night, when I heard a voice singing beneath my window. I looked out and managed to discern the figure of Gerald de Maur. Shortly afterwards a shot was heard and he fell wounded to the ground. I rushed from my room, in time to see a figure rush of(f); chuckling to himself, as he went. A second later, Gerald de Maur gave his last breath and died. They suspected Jack and arrested them."

Judge B:-

"And what do you say to that Prisoner?"

Jack:-

"Nothing, save that I am not guilty, and I am willing to swear that before a court of Ten Thousand Judges, or more if needs be"

Marie:-   "My beloved, I knew you were innocent. I am willing to bear you out."

Judge B:-   "It is now left to the jury to decide. Let them depart to their Consulting Room and be locked in until they can give us a satisfactory answer.(exit jury)

Marie:-   "Oh! That Gerald de Maur ever came to our village, all that he has brought with him is misery and pain. It is strange, but through all, love will find a way.

No 11   Song (Marie)   "Love finds a way"
In the springtime of the year
When the flowers begin to bloom
We are not shadowed by the thought,
Of winter and its gloom.
The Summer Sun shines brightly,
High high above the sky;
In the winter cold and drear,
Flowers fade and die.

Refrain:-   Love finds a way
To the brightness of the day.
From the darkness of the night,
To the morning, e'er so bright
Thro' the errors of this world,
Flies a banner unfurled,
For the brightness of the day,
Love will find a Way.

Verse II   The King Cups and the Marguerites,
Beside the flowing stream,
Lift up their little hands to catch
Each little bright sunbeam,
And thro' the cornfields hand in hand,
Two lovers pass their way;
In their search for happiness

And eternal day.

Judge B.:-   I care not for your arguments,
                The rime lays on his head;
                And no-one in this whole wideworld
                Will alter what I've said/

Chorus in unison:-   Ring, ring, Ring, ring,
                        Ring, ring the Curfew bell
                        Ring, ring, Ring, ring,
                        Ring, ring the prisoner's knell.
                        Whe day is turning into night,
                        Leaving behind the day so bright
                        Ring, ring, Ring, ring,
                        Ring, ring the Curfew bell

Curtain end of Act II

Act III

No. 16   Introduction and Duet (Marie & Jack) "Farewell"
                (in a prison Jack is seen)

Jack;_   The dreaded hour is drawing nigh
                In which from life I part

Marie:-   Say not. Oh! Well beloved,
                You know 't will break my heart.

Jack:-   For death no fears within me raise
                I know that you'll be with me;

Marie:-   Even to the bitter end,
                Ah! Yes I believe your
                Sweetheart I'll be with thee.

Refrain:-

Jack:-   Farewell,

Marie:-	Farewell,
Both:-	I'll meet you in Heav'n above;
Jack:-	Farewell,
Marie:-	Farewell,
Both:-	Farewell Oh! Farewell beloved Hopes I cherished do leave me And break my heart; Oh! Farewell beloved Oh! Farewell beloved We two must part.
Marie:_	Ah! No it cannot be, I will not part from thee; Whate'er befall (repeat) Repeat 1st section – where both ssing

Dialogue XI

Marie:-	"To think, that you go to your doom in half an hour. If only Cromwell would come before the Curfew rings we might appeal to his sense of Justice. Oh! I cannot bear it. If you die, I die also, for I cannot live without you. I will, once more, appeal, to the Bell Ringer, for here he comes." (enter Bell Ringer) do you know what love is?
Bell R.:-	"Eh! What did you say, for I am deaf?"
Marie:-	"I said, do you know what love is?
Bell R.:-	"Ay, ay, only too well."
Marie:- (aside)	"Here is a chance." (aloud) "Well, then, prove your knowledge by answering this question. Will you prevent the bell from ringing, for the prisoner is my lover, and he dies to-night, if the Curfew rings?"

Bell R.:- This twenty years I've rung that bell."

And I'll ring it now, tho' tis his knell."

Marie;- "What shall I do, what shall I do." (enter Squire C quietly behind Marie) "Ah! A plan has just struck me. I will enter the belfry, while there is no one about, climb the stairs and reach the Bell. The Bell Ringer who s deaf, will ring the Bell, and I will catch hold of it, thus preventing it from sounding."

Squire C:- How will that prevent the execution?"

Marie:- (aside) "Is it possible that I am discovered, I am almost afraid to lokk around." (looks around) (aloud) "Ah! It is you. What a fright I had. I really thought that all my plans had been discovered. You said how will it prevent the execution? That is simple. You bribe Father Joseph [135] to give you his outfit, and address in it yourself. He wears a cowl, so you will, and n-one will know the difference. In the meanwhile, I will carry out my plan. You will tell the Captain of the Guard,that it is an order of the Judges that the bell does not ring, and they will take Jack, back to his cell. Cromwell will come, and I will appeal to his sense of Jutice. It is, at least, an attempt to save Jack's life."

Squire C:- "I will away, for there is no time to be lost. In the meantime, you remain here, and watch your chance." (exit)

---

[135]   This part of the plotting does not ring true. The title Father is not used by 1 7th century Church of England clergy (Reverend Mister would be more likely). It is a more recent Catholic custom. Secondly, the use of a cowl relates to Roman Catholic pre-reformation monastic orders. Are Father Joseph, his priests and the church part of a Catholic monastic enclave? Surely Cromwell would have reacted differently if they were?

Marie:-   "I knew, that through it all, Love would find a
                            way.

No 17   Song (Marie)   "Love finds a way"
                            In the springtime of the year, etc and
                            refrain as in Act II for verse I and II
                            Repeat refrain (exit Marie) (enter Soldiers)

No 18 Soldiers March Song "March On"

Soldiers:-   March on, march on, March on then to victory
                            March on, march on, March on then to freedom
                            March on, march on, March on then to victory
                            March on, march on, March on then to death
                            March on, march on, March on then to victory
                            March on, march on, March on then to freedom
                            March on, march on, March on then to victory
                            March on, march on, March on.

Captain:-   Attention, quick march; Attention, quick march;
                            Obey my just commands, my just commands
                            Attention, quick march; Attention, quick march;
                            Left, right, left right, left, right, left,
                            Attention, quick march.

Soldiers:-   March on repeated

(enter priests)

No 19 Priests'Chorus "Prais to the Lord"

Priests:-   Praise to the Lord
                            The Lord, the God of all;
                            All nations down before him fall.
                            Praise to the Lord
                            Who reigns enthron'd above;
                            Praise to the Lord
                            The God of Love (repeat)

Marie:- (sings from the tower of the church)

Father in heaven, etc (as in Act II)

Recit (Squire Courtenay) (Aside)
        "Oh! Heavens, 'tis she,
        We are undone.
        (aloud) Who(m) is there?
        Captain of the Guard
        The tower must be searched.

(Squire Courtenay)   No time must be lost,
        The Curfew must ring;
        Delay until afterwards,
        Your search of the Tower.

No 21   March

Jack is brought to centre of stage, and soldiers fix their guns to shoot.)

No 22   Song (Jack)   "The Shades of Night"
                      Repeat as in Act II

Dialogue XII

Capt:-   "This is strange. The Curfew has not ring."

Squire C.   "No need of being alarmed Captain. I thought it would happen like this. It is undoubtedly, an order of the Judges that the execution is postponed."

Capt:-   "Ah! Yes, I believe you(')r(e) right. Well, anyway, the Curfew does not ring, and the prisoner does not die" (to soldiers) "Take him back to his cell, he is safer there."

Squire C.:-   "It is done. It is done. My son will be saved.

No 23   March (during which Jack is taken back to his cell.)

Dialogue XIII

(enter Cromwell) (enter Chorus one by one)

Chorus:-   "Cromwell, Cromwell, hurrah, hurrah

Crom:-   "My friends, how are you all assembled here?"

Capt.: -   "There was to be an execution at the ringing of the Curfew, but, as the Bell did not ring, the Prisoner did not die."

Crom.:-   "Very remarkable indeed. How was it, then that the Bell did not ring?"

Capt:-   "Father Joseph here says that it was an order of the Judges, and by the way, Father Joseph what became of that voice in the tower?"

(enter Marie from Church door, and bleeding)

Marie:-   "Cromwell, Cromwell, thank God you've come."

Crom:-   "Why? What's this?

Marie:-   "Listen, listen, I have a tale to tell you. I am Mare Blanche, the beloved of the prisoner. Not very long ago, there came to this village a French Lord by the name of Gerald de Maur."

Crom:-   "Gerald de Maur. The very man."

Marie:-   "He brought with him nothing but misery and crime. He took a liking to me, and serenaded me beneath my window. He was shot, and Jack Courtenay as accused. He was tried, and they found him guilty of the crime. He was sentenced to death at the ringing of the curfew this evening. I, and his father, conceived a plan between us. We planned, that he should bribe Father Joseph for his outfit and come here in his stead, so that he might make excuses to the Captain for the Bell not

	ringing. Then I entered the Belfry, and climbed the stairs, until I came to Bell. The old Bellringer was deaf, so when the Bell moved, I hung to the tongue and prevented it from sounding. Now, I am here before you. I cast myself upon your mercy. Spare him, and I will do anything for you, even die or you."
Crom:-	"No, no my girl you should be restored to you lover, even if he did commit the crime, but I happen to know that he is innocent. Now, you should listen to my story. A little while ago King Charles was executed, and on the scaffold, he confessed that he was the murderer of Gerald de Maur, [136] so that frees your lover from any guilt, and to your bravery there shall be a monument, for never I am sure was there ever braver woman in English History."
Marie:-	"I do it for love, and nothing else."
Crom:-	"Let the prisoner be restored to his sweetheart." (Jack is brought from his cell. He rushed to Marie and takes her in his arms) "Young sir, you have no one to thank, but this maiden, and your father for your prescence (sic) here at this moment. (Jack rushes to his father, and they both embrace) And now-----"
Mdme G:-	"Stay, I have a confession to make. A long while ago I married a Lord by the name of Gerald Felding. We lived, happily together, rearing one child. Then came a matter of treason. My husband was accused, but, as no evidence was

---

[136] Again there are historical anomalies. The King was actually in custody as noted in Act I. This part of the plot is not sufficiently thought through. Was some Cavalier involved in G de M's earlier alleged treason and so rather than the King himself became the murderer?

brought up against him he was banished for ever from the country. He sought sanctuary, in the court of Louis, where he soon came into favour, adopting the name of Lord Gerald de Maur." (Chorus move back in horror) "He thought he would like to see me once again and risked his life in coming to England, where I was living, away from my daughter Marie Blanche ------------."

Marie:-   "Me, your daughter? Thank heaven I have found my other."

(rushes to her and embraces her.)

Mdme G.:-   "As I said, he came to England with the purpose of seeing us. He serenaded Marie, with the purpose of finding out if she was true to her love as he had been, but, alas, he was shot," (to Cromwell) "As you say, by King Charles I. I kept the secret from Marie, thinking perhaps it was best." (to Chorus) "Now perhaps you understand why I opposed the Squire in the trial."

Papa O.:-   "Yes, yes, We all understand, Popsy Wopsy, we all understand."

Eliz:-   "Popsy Wopsy ? Why Popsy Wopsy?"

PapaO.:-   "Well, because we are going to get married."

Chorus: "Married?"

Papa O. & Mdme G.:- "Yes, married."

Charles:-   "I congratulate you, Papa."

Papa O.:-   "No need, I am sure, I mean, thank you very much."

Eliz.:-   "And I congratulate you, Madame."

Mdme G.:-   "Oh! Thanks very much, and we're going to have a little cottage in the woods, aren't we dear?"

Papa O:-   "Oh! Yes, love. Two of them if you like." (aside) "Oh! Dash it (aloud) I mean one; will rose and jasmine and pinks--------."

Mdme G.:-   "And sows."

Papa O.:-   "I didn't say pigs, I said pinks."

Mdme G.:-   "Oh" never mind we'll have everything."

Chorus:-   "No."

Mdme G.:-   "We're going to call it our cottage of love."

No 24 (Mdme G & Papa Oldham)   "There'll be"

Verse I

Papa O:-   The scent of flowers round about you,
                        Fill the air with perfume sweet;

Mdme G:-   The scent of flowers round about you,
                        Nothing can their perfume beat.

Refrain (both)

                        There'll be a horse and a cow,
                        And a little bow-wow-wow,
                        In our cottage of love.
                        There'll be a pig and a sow,
                        Underneath the Chestnut Bough,
                        In our cottage of love.
                        In our cottage of love.
                        We'll have pretty rose growing round the door,
                        Pansies, stocks, ~~chrysto~~ chrysanthemums and pinks galore;
                        Here I'll be King, and you'll be queen, of the tardy forest green

	In our cottage of love.
Chorus:-	repeat refrain
Verse II	
Papa O.:-	I love you more than I can tell you And that's something true;
Mdme G.;-	I love you more than I can tell you And that's something too.
Refrain (both)	(repeat refrain and then chorus)
Dialogue XIV	
Crom.:-	"And now, all mysteries cleared away, the Curfew, shall ring for the marriage of Marie Blanche, and Jack Courtenay."
Chorus:-	"Hurrah, hurrah, long live the Curfew."
No 25	Finale

APPENDIX 4

CHRONOLOGY

Includes list of tours, premières of revues, musicals, broadcasts, concerts, records, and release dates of films.

N.B. Compositions were obviously done at unspecified times before the date of release of films, revues, musicals or published songs. In addition, there was more mainly uncharted time for setting productions and rehearsing concerts, films and stage shows, also tailoring or adding songs for specific occasions and preparing for recordings and concerts.

1914

24 May	born 11 Grandison Street, Briton Ferry, Glamorgan
1919	
c. early September	family moves to Tynewydd; started Dunraven Primary School, Tynewydd Treherert and plays *I'm Forever Blowing Bubbles*' on piano
c. 1920-1	moves to Neath - 2 Arthur St. Neath and started Gnoll Primary School

1922

February   sends Cantata to Princess Mary on her wedding
                                  to Viscount Lascelles

1923

? September   starts Neath Intermediate School; wrote c. 30
                                  songs while there and an operetta

1925   a pupil of Seymour Parrott

1926

                                  A foxtrot composed by Harry played at Empire
                                  Cinema
                                  sends letter to publisher, Lawrence Wright
                                  about publishing his songs

1927

? at end of Easter term writes scenario, words and music for operetta
                                  'The Curlew' given at school
24 May   starts Neath Grammar School

1928

8 April   concert at Bethany English Presbyterian
                                  Church, Glynneath
14 April   concert of his music held in Wesley Methodist
                                  Church Neath
                                  works at getting his music published; music
                                  played in London and broadcast

1930

30 November   becomes member of Royal College of Organists

1932

February   contract for publishing from Horatio Nicholls
                                  left school;

Summer	sits Matriculation exam and leaves school
September	*Looking on the Bright Side* - Harry's first film for Gracie

1933

April/ May	revue **Walk This Way** ends
14 September	*This Week of Grace* - Gracie film
	Gracie buys 'Greentrees', Hampstead. Harry lives in almost as a 'family' member; and 'Il Postino', renamed as 'La Canzone del Mare' Harry visits often
18 December	A selection of music from *This Week of Grace* is recorded by Edison Bell Winner record company

1934

	Sing As We Go - Gracie film
	moves into Gracie's 'Greentrees', 36 Hampstead Road, Finchley;
	some weekends at Gracie's parents' house in 29, Telscombe Cliffs Way

1935

March	reception in Neath for father, mother and Glenys leaving Neath to move to Swansea
4 August	*Look Up and Laugh* - Gracie film
28 October	*No Limit* - first George Formby film
21 November	sets off for tour of South Africa with Gracie sailed out on Union Castle 'Windsor Castle'; gave concert on board

1936

7 January	visits 'East Geduld' Gold Mine, Springs and the Cullinan diamond mine Johannesburg
Late March	expected back from South Africa
26 March	sails from Cape Town home to Southampton; concert on board *Stirling Castle*

30 March	BBC Northern Programme (441 metres) 10 pm BBC Variety Orchestra under Larry Ross - Gracie sings with Harry at piano
25 May	Gracie broadcasts to Australia with Harry accompanying her.
1 August	***Keep Your Seats Please*** - George Formby film
Winter	Holidays with Gracie and her parents at St Moritz

1937

5 February	Gracie attends opening of the opening of Black's Regal Cinema, Gateshead
10 February	*I See Ice* - George Formby film
5 March	sails on 'Queen Mary' from Southampton to New York with Gracie (as Mrs Salinger)
17 March	*BBC Western Programme* (373.1 metres) broadcasts a selection of his music, arranged by Leonard Morris and Garfield Philipps and played *by Garfield Philipps Quartet*
April	***The Show Goes On*** - Gracie film
22 May	9.45 pm - accompanies Gracie in 'Starlight' TV programme, broadcast from Alexandra Palace; BBC Television Orchestra conducted by Hyam Greenbaum.
Mid-July	goes with his mother Rosina to see ***The Show Goes On***
19 July	Rosina sees him accompanying Gracie at Palladium
August	To Capri to prepare for next film broadcasts with Gracie from *Radio Luxembourg*

1938

13 February	2 charity concerts (Grand Theatre and Central Hall) with Gracie at Derby (he joined in repartee)
28 May	accompanies Gracie on stage in show finale at *London Palladium.*
3 July	***We're Going to Be Rich-*** released Gracie film

August	***Lassie from Lancashire*** -Marjorie Browne film
10 November	**Regal Zonophone** recording with Gracie
19 November	sails from Southampton on SS. *Normandie* with Gracie
November	***It's in the Air*** - George Formby film
24 December	***Penny Paradise*** - Betty Driver film
December	***Keep Smiling*** - Gracie film

1939

17 February	*Umbrella Man* for **Regal Zonophone** recording with Gracie and her brother Tommy Harry (piano) and orchestra
Before June	***Shipyard Sally*** completed the last Gracie film for which Harry provides songs
30 July	Solo record released for **Regal Zonophone;** concert with Gracie at Blackburn before she sailed to Capri
20 October	release of ***Shipyard Sally***
14 November	***Black Velvet*** – Harry's first George Black revue
17 November	Gracie and Harry (piano), recording *Wish Me Luck*, *Old Violin* and *When I Grow Too Old to Dream* (with *Walter Walter*) for **Regal Zonophone**
9 December - new Year	3 weeks in France for NAAFI, accompanying Gracie's concerts in Douai and Arras
14 December	***Sailors Three*** – a Tommy Trinder film
22 December	***Haw Haw*** – George Black Crazy Gang revue
25 December	pm - *BBC* Gracie broadcasts from war front with Harry as accompanist and Jack Payne and his orchestra

1940

5 January	Gracie returns from France
2 February	Harry as soloist in variety concert at *Colston Hall*, Bristol
6 February	*BBC Forces Programme* 12.30 am. Half hour music by Harry, billed as 'accompanist-in-ordinary' to Gracie

8 February	12.30 Harry tells Lesley Perowne some of his life story and some of his music was played
19 March	*Come Out to Play* – George Black revue
April	tours France with Gracie as part of ENSA concerts
March	Gracie goes off to USA to get married to Monty
24 June	sails on Canadian Pacific *Duchess of Bedford* from Southampton to Montreal to join Gracie who had arrived on 13
July	goes with Gracie to her parent's house in Santa Monica
Late July	3 concerts in British Columbia and gala in Vancouver
7 August	concerts at Eaton auditorium in Toronto/ Calgary *Top of the World* – George Black revue bombed and therefore closes after 4 days
16 August	concert at 8.30 pm at Regina, Saskatchewan (branch of Canadian Navy League)
21 August	touring version of *Black Velvet* starting at *Nottingham Empire Theatre*
12 September	at Ottawa

1941

March 9	*Gangway* - George Black review
10 August	officially enlists and is posted to *His Majesty's Life Guards Band* under Col. Albert Lemoine (see details below for band recordings and broadcasts)
17 August	ENSA concert at *Royal Albert Hall*, accompanying Gracie
7 November	9.20 - 10.00 pm *BBC Forces Programme* broadcast is postponed due to Harry's illness rescheduled for 21 November
21 November	Home service 9.20 broadcast 'The Story of Gracie Fields' recalled by Harry and Bert Aza
6 December	Gracie in Winnipeg
17 December	*Happidrome* – stage version at *London Palladium*

1942

18 February	***Full Swing*** Harry's first George Black musical co-written with George Posford starts provincial preview
16 April	***Full Swing*** London first night
8 May	***Big Top*** George Black revue
June	***Suspected Person*** David Farrar/Patricia Roc film
c. 7 August	elected to committee of *Performing Rights Society*
2- 8 August	plays piano with *Her Majesty's Life Guard Band* under Lt.-Col Lane Fox each afternoon in Montpellier Gardens
14-21 September	Given leave
16 September	Writes insert song for ***Belle of New York*** at *London Coliseum*
7 November	***Best Bib & Tucker*** George Black revue Travels to Santa Monica and stays at Gracie's.

1943

18 January	***We'll Meet Again*** - Vera Lynn film
6 March	ball held in Gloucester Guildhall for Gloucester City Police in aid of the Red Cross Prisoner of War Fund and Longford Children's Hospital
1 May	***The Lisbon Story*** - musical with provincial preview
7 June	***Happidrome*** - MGM film of BBC radio series
1 July	***The Knight is Bold*** - George Black musical complete score
11 November	Grand Armistice Ball held in Gloucester by Dance band section of His Majesty's Life Guards, with Harry as soloist. Becomes exhausted again

1944

7 February	***Bell Bottom George*** - last Formby film
21 March	*Salute the Soldier* Pageant – 3 weeks at Stoll Theatre London, then provincal tour to provincial cities including Leeds and Sheffield.

20 April	***The Rest Is Silence*** - Harold Purcell play opens
10 June	stays at Sheriff's Private Hotel
18 July	***It Happened One_Sunday*** - Robert Beatty film
18 July	concert in Lewis Town Hall
20 August	set out from Gosport for 6-month Guards Band tour of liberated North West Europe, travelling c. 2500 miles through Normandy, Belgium and Holland
2 October	***Jenny Jones*** - George Black musical

1945

9 March	returns to UK
May	doesn't travel with Gracie to Australia; end of their permanent professional relationship as her accompanist, cf song *Peter the Penguin*
4 and 5 August	plays piano in His Majesty's Life Guards Band as inaugural concert (Saturday afternoon) for Sports Festival as well as two on (Sunday afternoon) at festival in Montpellier Gardens, Cheltenham
20 August	travels to Paris for 25 August remembrance of Victory Parade
31 August	returns from France
3 October	***Fine Feathers*** - George Black musical

1946

21 February	***The Lisbon Story*** - film of musical
18 May	Demobbed acquires mews flat at 11 Harriet Walk Knightsbridge
26 September	***The Shephard Show*** revue

| **1947** | member of *Savage Club* |

1948

Several songs published

1949

19 April	***Her Excellency*** Cecily Courtneidge musical, co-written with Manning Sherwin
24 May	***Maytime in Mayfair*** Anna Neagle musical film
Summer	BBC 'Welsh Rarebit' broadcast with Harry and his music

1950

6 March	Songwriter's Guild of Great Britain Annual concert
31 July to 30 September	***Dear Miss Phoebe***
14 August	***Blue For a Boy or What shall we do with the Body?*** Provincial pre-view tour Fred Emney musical
6-11 November	***Lisbon Story***, produced by Neath Operatic Society
10 November	Harry at civic dinner in Neath
30 November	***Blue For a Boy or What shall we do with the Body?*** London Fred Emney musical - 8 songs

1951

23 January	Harry's father dies in Swansea and
29 January	is buried in Oystermouth cemetery
4 March	Songwriter's Guild of Great Britain Annual concert
3 May	march for opening of Festival of Britain
1952	
Summer	***Glorious Days*** pre-London run in Manchester 6 weeks; then Glasgow; Bristol; Coventry and
November-December	its final pre-London run in Edinburgh

1953

28 February	***Glorious Days*** - opens in London
9 March	Songwriter's Guild of Great Britain Annual concert

1954

7 March	Songwriter's Guild of Great Britain Annual concert
23 September	in Italy at Rome on holiday
21 December	*Lilacs in the Spring* - Anna Neagle musical film of *Glorious Days*

1955

20 March	Songwriter's Guild of Great Britain concert
c. mid September	Article for 'Red Letter Days' on Gracie *Now and Forever* Janet Scott film – 1 title song (released **21/2/1956**) preparing 2 other musicals, *Marry Me Margaret, Caroline*, plus a possible Ivor Novello adaptation
14 October	dies alone in 13 Harriet Mews, Knightsbridge of perforated gastric ulcer
18 October	is buried beside his father in Oystermouth Cemetery Swansea

1964

29 March	his mother died in Swansea
1 April	buried beside her son and husband Oystermouth Cemetery Swansea

1973

February	his sister Glenys dies and
1 March	is cremated and ashes scattered over burial place of brother, father and mother in Oystermouth Cemetery Swansea

2011

August	Marjorie (Billie) dies aged 99 years and
26 August	is cremated and ashes scattered over burial place of brother sister father and mother in Oystermouth Cemetery Swansea

APPENDIX 5

BIBLIOGRAPHY

Allsobrook, David Ian, 1992, *Music for Wales: Walford Davies and the National Council for Music 1918-1941,* University of Wales Press

The Argus (Melbourne) 15 June 1940

Bath Chronicle and Gazette, 10 June 1944

Christopher Bray, 2010, *Sean Connery the Measure of the Man,* Faber and Faber

Breese, Charlotte, 1999, *Hutch,* Bloomsbury

Bret, David, 1995, *The Real Gracie Fields,* J R Books Ltd

Bret, David, 1999, George Formby, Robson Books Ltd

BBC Radio interview with Harry by Leslie Perowne on 7 February 1940

BBC Radio programme 'Welsh Rarebit' dedicated to Harry and his music. Summer 1949

Andrew Everett MA

BBC Interview with Harry's sister Billie' David, 1990

Burgess, Muriel (with Tommy Keen), 1980, *Gracie Fields,* W H Allen

Cheltenham Chronicle

Collen, Jean, 2006, *Sweethearts of Song, Anne Ziegler & Webster Booth,* Lulu

1923 Colliery Year Book and Coal Trades Directory.

Coward, Noel p. vii in Raymond Mander and Joe Mitchenson, 1971, *Revue – a story in pictures,* Peter Davies

Derby Daily Telegraph 5 February

Dundee Evening Telegraph, 7 February 1940

Evening Chronicle, % February 1937

Evening Telegraph, Perth, 13 November 1950

Fields, Gracie, 1960, *Sing as We Go, The Autobiography of Gracie Fields,* Frederick Mulle

Fisher, John, 1975, *The Entertainers - George Formby,* Philip Oates

Ganzl, Kurt, 1986, *The British Musical Theatre* vol 2 Macmillan

Gloucester Citizen 6 March 1942 and 8 November 1943

Gloucester Echo, 3 and 6 August 1945

www.billhanks.co.uk (no longer operational)

Household Cavalry Museum and Archive Records

Hulbert, Jack, 1975, *The Little Woman's Always right,* WH Allen

Lawn, George R, 1995, *Music in State Clothing the Story of the Kettledrummers, Trumpeters and the Band of the Life Guards,* Lee Cooper

Marshall, Michael, 1978, *Top Hat And Tails,* Elm Tree

Mitchinson, Joe & Mander, Raymond, 1969, *Musical Comedy,* P Davies

Moules, Joan, 1997, *Our Gracie, the Biography of Dame Gracie Fields,* Summersdale

Neagle Anna, 1974, *There will always be to-morrow,* W H Allen

The New Groves Dictionary of Music and Musicians, 2001, 2nd Edition, Oxford University Press

Nottingham Evening Post, 7 November 1941

The Official Gracie Fields website graciefields.org

Oystermouth Cemetary records for the Davies family

Plimmer, Martin & King, Brian, 2005, *Beyond Co-incidence,* Icon Books

Randall, Alan & Seaton, Ray, 1974 *George Fromby – a biography,* W H Allen

Red Letter Days, *The Gracie I Know* c. Mid-September 1955 interview with Harry,

Self, Geoffrey, 1986, *In Town Tonight,- a centenary study of the life and music of Eric Coates,* Thames Publishing

South Wales Daily Post, (c. February/ March) 1932 interview

South Wales Evening Post, 15 October 1955

South Wales News, 27 July 1937

'Times' 1/11/1955 obituary

Western Mail 15 October 1955

Yorkshire Evening Post, 21 November 1941

INDEX

**Actual non-stage   or additional names in bold and brackets
n = page of footnotes**

Askey, Arthur (**Bowden**), 1900-1982, comedian, 80, 82, 128

Asta (**Skippy**), 1931-?, canine actor, 70

Aza, Bert, 1884-1953, Gracie's agent, 20, 25, 45, 91, 91n, 222

Banks, Monty (**Mario Bianchi**), 1897-1950, Italian actor producer/ director, 45, 47, 50, 52, 63, 66, 70, 73, 74, 80-2, 141, 165, 166, 167, 168, 172, 222

Barrett, Mary, 1904-1978, Gracie's secretary-companion, 38, 63, 80

Beaumont, Roma, 1893-1970, singer and lyricist, 31, 71, 77, 165

Belmore, Bertha, 1882-1959, actress,

Black, George, 1890-1953, impresario, 55, 75-6, 77-8, 85, 96, 100, 112, 118, 168, 169, 170, 172, 173, 221, 222-23 224

Booth, Webster, 1902-1980, tenor, 87-8, 128, 140, 170, 232

Brandon, Philip, 1898-1982, producer, 100-1, 172, 173

Browne, Coral, 1913-1991, Australian character actress, 66-7

Browne, Marjorie, 1910-1990, singer-dancer , 67

Buchanan, Jack (**Walter John**), 1891-1957, dancer, 92, 123

Burke, Marie, 1894-1988, actress, 127

Burke, Patricia, 1917-2003, singer/actress, Marie's daughter, 29, 94, 95, 105-109, 117, 126, 148

Butler, Ralph, 1886-1969, lyricist, 77, 78, 168

Byrd, Bretton, 1904-1959, h conductor and composer- music arranger, 31, 36, 66, 166, 167, 173

Campbell-Hunter, Roma, lyricist, 32, 53, 65, 75, 77, 91, 167, 168, 169, 173

Cantor, Eddie (**Isidore Itzkowitz**), 1892-1964, American comedy star, 58, 61

Carstairs, John Paddy (**John Nelson**), 1910-1970, film producer, 67, 166

De Cassalis, Jeanne, 1899-1966, South African actress, 86

Chaplin, Charlie (**Charles Spencer**), 1889-1977, comic actor, 59, 128

Charlot, André (**Eugène Maurice**), 1882-1956, French actor/impresario, 16

Coates, Eric, 1886–1957, <u>composer</u> of <u>light music</u>, 12-13, 12n, 13n, 28, 86, 133, 133n, 233

Cochrane, CB (**Charles Blake**), 1872-1951, actor/ impresario, 16, 85, 94, 171

Connery, Sean (**Thomas**), 1930 ??, actor, 140-1

Courtneidge, Cicely, 1892-1980, Australian comedy actress, x, 91, 129-30, 225

Craxton, (**Thomas**) Harold (**Hunt**), 1885-1971, concert pianist, 23, 44, 81

Coward, Noel, 1899-1970, playwright and composer, 28, 31, 39, 76, 76n, 232

Cutts, Graham, 1885-1958, director, 36

Daniels, Bebe, 1901-1971, American actress, 78, 87

David, Geoffrey, 1901-1994, Harry's brother-in-law, 46-7, 139, 144-45

David, Marjorie ('Billie') (née **Davies**), 1911-2011, Harry's sister, xi, 2, 3, 18, 27, 33, 46, 57, 129, 139, 143, 143n, 145, 145-48, 217, 219, 226

Davies, David John, 1880-1951, Harry's father, 2, 3, 8, 18, 20, 46-7, 57, 58, 59, 129, 139-40, 144, 146,147, 217, 219, 225

Davies, Glenys Kathleen, 1911-1974, Harry's sister, 2, 3, 18, 46, 57, 58, 129, 139, 143, 144, 146, 217, 219, 226

Davies, Henry Walford, 1869- 1941, composer, 8-9, 11-12, 30, 81, 218

Davies, Rosina (née **Parr**), 1883-1964, Harry's mother 2, 3, 8, 11, 18, 20, 46, 57, 62, 129, 139, 145, 146, 217, 219, 220, 226

Dean, Basil, 1888-1978, film director, 15, 36, 41, 45, 52, 56, 68, 80, 164, 169

Dempster, Hugh, 1900-1987, actor, 168,

Desmond, Florence, 1905-1993, actress, 46

Donlevy, Brian, 1899-1972, Ulster-born Hollywood actor, 66-7

Drayton, Alfred, 1881-1949, character actor, 47, 101

Driver, Betty, 1920-2011, singing-actress, 69-70, 225

Ellis, Vivian, 1903-1990, composer, 28, 91 150

Elvey, Maurice, 1887-1967, film producer, 15, 39, 167

Emney, Fred, 1900-1980, comic actor, 94, 136-8, 225

Farjeon, Herbert, 1887-1915, lyricist and theatre critic, 23, 81, 92, 171

Farrar, David, 1936-95, actor, 95

Fenoulhet, Paul 1906-79, conductor, 92, 126

Fields, Gracie, (**Grace Stansfield**), 1898-1979, singer, comedienne and actress, ix, x, 15-22, 19n, 20n, 21n, 22n, 26-7, 27n, 29, 30, 32-3, 35-44, 39n, 44n 45, 46-54, 50n, 55-62, 55n, 56n, 57n, 61n, 62n, 63-71, 64n, 65n, 73-4, 74n, 76, 79, 80, 80n, 81, 82, 83-4, 84n, 86, 88, 89, 91n, 92, 93, 93n, 97, 115, 120-1, 129, 143, 146, 149, 167, 219-22, 224, 225, 228

Fields Tommy (**Stansfield**), c. 1908-1988, Gracie's brother, 17, 22, 27, 35, 47, 50-1, 56, 70, 221

Finck, Herman (**van der Vinck**), 1872-1939, composer, 94

Flynn, Errol, 1909-59, Australian-born Hollywood star, 140

Foley, Adrian (**Gerald 9th Baron**), 1923-2012, lyricist and composer, 96-7, 172

Foort, Reginald, 1893-1980, theatre organist, 13

Formby, George junior (**George Hoy**), 1904-1961, comedian x, 27, 28, 30, 45-6, 52, 55, 64-6, 65n, 68, 69-70, 80, 85, 92, 111-2, 111n, 219-21, 224, 225, 226, 227, 231, 232, 233

France, Anatole (**François-Anatole Thibault**), 1844 -1924, French novelist, 119

Frankel, Ben (**Benjamin**), 1906-1973, composer, 81, 95

Franklin, Gretchen, 1911-2005 character actress, 94

Gay, Noel (**Reginald Armitage**), 1898-1954, composer, 28, 78, 86,

German, (**Jones**), Edward, 1862-1936, composer, 12-13, 13n, 28, 132

Gibbons, Carrol, 1903-54, American conductor and pianist, 36, 167

Gordon, Barbara, lyricist, 32, 82, 87, 93, 94, 103-5, 169, 170, 171 174, 178

Gordon, Gavin, 1901- 1983, American actor, 127

Graves, (**Lord**) Peter, 1911-1994, aristocrat and actor, 130, 140

Gray, Eddie (**Edward Earl**), 1898-1963, comedian, 70, 126

Greenbaum, Hyam, 1901-1942, violinist and conductor, 61

Grey, Clifford, 1887-1941, lyricist, 52, 53, 165

Gwenn, Edmund, 1877-1959, film actor, 69

Hale, Sonnie (**John Robert Hale-Monro**), 1902-1959, theatre and film actor and director, 82, 103

Hare, Robertson, 1891-1979, comic actor, 99

Hassall, Christopher, 1912-1963, lyricist, 32, 128, 131-35, 136, 142, 145-6, 145n, 150, 177, 178, 179

Hayden, Walford, 1890-1982, conductor, 68

Hearne, Richard, 1919-1979, comic actor, 126

Holloway, Stanley, 1890-1982, comic actor, 42, 49

Howard, Sydney, 1885-1946, actor, 73

Hulbert, Claude, 1900-1964, character actor, x, 86,

Hulbert, Jack, 1892-1978, character actor, x, 93, 103, 103n, 232

Hutch (**Hutchinson Leslie**), 1892-1978, Grenada-born singer and pianist, x, 44, 92-3, 231

Hyson, Dorothy, 1914-1996, actress, 42

Irving, Ernest, 1878-1953, music director and arranger,15, 31, 36, 42, 45, 51, 56, 69, 86, 164, 165 166, 167, 168, 170, 171, 174

Jackson, Sir John, 1868-1939, Deputy Lord Lieutenant of Lancashire, 68

Kirkwood, Pat, 1921-2007, actress and singer, 77, 82, 85

Laurie, John, 1897-1980, character actor, 86

Leigh, Vivien, 1913-1967, Indian born actress, 47

Lemoine, Albert, Life Guard's Band Director of Music, 19??-1997, 89, 96, 101, 113-8, 122-3, 222

Levy, Louis, 1893-1957, film music director 73-4, 82, 172, 173

Lieven, Albert, 1906-1971, English actor. 106

Lillie, Beatrice, 1894-1989, Canadian-born character actress, 94

Lipton, Celia, 1923-2011, singer and actress, 75

Lister, Eve, 1913-1997, actress, 136

Littler, Emile, 1903-1885, impresario, 946, 103, 136, 142, 178

Livesey, Jack, 1901-, actor, 70, 105

Loder, John, 1898-1988, actor, 36, 41, 52

Lynn, Vera (**Vera Margaret Welch**), 1917- ??, 80, 102, 223

Lynne, Carol (**Helen Violet Caroline Hayman**), 1918-2008, singing-actress, 77, 121

Lyon, Ben, 1901-1979, American actor, 78-9, 87

Mackey, (**Thomas Percival**) Montague, 1895 - 1950, conductor, composer and music arranger, 39, 41, 163

McLaglen, Victor, 1886-1959, Hollywood film star, 66-7

Maltby, HF (**Henry Francis**), 1880-1963, South African actor and screenwriter, 52

Matthews, Jessie, 1907-1981, actress, 81

Melford, Austin, 1884-1971, screen writer and actor, 85-6, 136

Messini (also **Mesene**), Jimmy, songwriter, 71, 167

Millar, Ronald, 1919-1998, actor/writer, 119, 121

Miller, Max, (**Thomas Henry Sargent**), 1894-1963, comedian, 78

Mitchell, Julian, 1888-1954, actor, 69

More, Kenneth, 1914-1982, actor, 36

Munro, Ronnie, 1897-1989, music director, 67, 166

Neagle, Anna (**Florence Marjorie Robinson**), 1904-1986, actress, 130, 140, 225, 230, 233

Nesbitt, Robert, 1906-1995, producer, 87, 168

Nares, Owen, 188?-1943, actor, 56

Nicholls, Horatio (also Everett Linton and as publisher **Lawrence Wright**), 1888-1964, publisher and lyricist, 5, 13, 25, 28, 54, 58, 71, 150, 164, 167, 170, 171, 218

Novello, Ivor(**David Ivor Davies**), actor, playwright and composer, 28, 106, 145, 150, 230

O'Dea, Jimmy, 1899-1965, Irish actor, 69

Oliver, Vic (**Viktor Oliver Samek**), 1881-1964, Austrian musician and comic ,77

O'Neill (**Allgood**), Maire, 1887-195, Irish character actress, 69

O'Shea, Tessie, 1913-1995, comedienne, 92, 126

Park, Phil, 1907-1987, lyricist, 31, 74, 78, 85, 86, 87, 89, 111, 120, 123, 168, 169, 170, 173, 175 179

Parr-Davies, Harry, 1914-1955, composer and pianist, ix, x, 2-14, 7n, 8n, 12n, 15-23,18n, 19n, 20n, 21n, 22n, 23n, 25-33, 35-44, 39n, 43n, 44n, 45-54, 55-62, 65n, 57n, 59n, 61n, 62n, 63-71, 65n, 73-82, 83-7, 89-99, 91n, 93n, 97n, 100-1, 103, 105-110 111n, 111-24, 112n,113n, 118n, 128-32, 123n, 126-30, 126n, 128n 131-37, 139-46, 140n, 143n, 145n, 150-51, 160-79, 181-185, 217-226

Pavlov, (**Lilian**) Muriel, 1921-, actress 36, 42

Peerce, Jan (**Jacob Joshua Pincus Perelmuth**), 1904-1984, American tenor, 49

Perrott, Seymour FRCO, 1890-1974, organist,4-5, 8, 12, 30, 81, 139, 218

Perowne, Leslie (**Arthur William Thomson**), 1906-1997, BBC Head of Music, 8n, 12n, 23n, 81, 222

Pettingell, Frank, 1891-1960, character actor, 40

Pitts, Archie (**Archibald Selinger**), 1885-1940, Gracie's manager and 1st husband, 15-16, 20, 21, 26, 74

Pola, Eddie (**Sydney Edward Pollascek**), 1907-1995, American lyricist and composer, 31, 56, 81, 165

Posford, George 1906-1976, composer, 91

Priestley, JB (**John Boynton**) 1894-1984, social writer, 36, 41, 47

Purcell, Harold (**Vousden**) 1907-1977, lyricist and playwright, 32, 102, 107-111,114, 118-20, 126, 128, 129, 136, 142, 145, 150, 173, 178, 179, 224

Raynor, Minnie 1869- 1941, singing actress, 40,

Reed, Carol, 1906-1976, film director, 68, 166

Riscoe, Arthur, 1895-1954, English actor, 126, 227

Roc, Patricia, (**Felicia Herold**) 1915-?, English actress, 95

Rossini, Nino (**Lorenzo**) 1902-65, accordionist, 22, 27, 50-1, 70

Sandler, Albert, 1905-1948, popular violinist, 12, 22

Sim, Alastair, 1900-76, actor, 51

Somers, (**William**) Debroy, 1890-1952, Irish born music arranger and conductor, 31 78, 88, 105, 17

Stamp-Taylor, Enid, 1904-1969, singer-actress, 52, 98, 104

Stone, Lew, 1898-1969, orchestrator and band leader, 91

Stuart, John, 1898-1979, actor, 56

Tate, Arthur, 1870-1950, British composer, 94

Tauber, Richard, 1891-1948, Austrian tenor, 125-6

Thomas, Basil, 1912-55, lyricist, 32, 82, 89, 94, 103-5, 128, 169, 172, 174

Thompson, Hal, 1899-1966, actor, 67

Toye, Wendy (**Beryl May Jessie**), 1917-2010, choreographer, 127

Trinder, Tommy, 1909-1989, comedian, 85-6, 87, 96, 221

Vincent, Robbie, 1895-1968, actor, 92

Wagstaffe, Elsie (**Lilian**), 1899-1985, actress, 67

Wakefield, Duggie (**Douglas**), 1899-1951, actor, 17, 22, 23, 27, 35, 40, 47

Wakefield (nee **Stansfield**), Edith, Gracie's sister, Duggie Wakefield's wife, 35, 52

Walsh, Kay, 1911-2005, actress, 65,

Whitty, May, (**Mary Louise Webster**), 1965-1948, actress, 51

Widdop, Walter, 1892-1949, Wagnerian heldentenor, 44

Wilding Michael (**Charles Gauntlett**), 1912-1979, actor, 86, 130

Williams, Charles (**Izaac Cozerbreit**), 1893-1978, composer-conductor, 31, 36, 100, 112, 172, 173, 174, 175

Wilton, Robb, 1881-1957, comedian 38, 47,

Wylie Julian (**Julian Ulrich Mettenberg Samuelson**), 1878-1934, business impresario, 12, 18

Zeigler, Anne (**Irene Eastwood**), soprano, 87-88, 112, 140, 170, 232